TRANSFORMING YOUR COMPANY'S CULTURE:
Creating EternalROI™

*An Introductory Guide for Company Leaders
to Create Eternal Value Through
a Caring Company Culture*

TRANSFORMING YOUR COMPANY'S CULTURE: CREATING ETERNALROI™

Designed by The Brand Leader, 18 S. Markley Street Suite B, Greenville, SC 29601; 864.281.1323; thebrandleader.com

Published by WOR-K-SHIP Publishing, 1790 Dewberry Road, Spartanburg, SC 29307; 866.570.1229; hwaw.com

ISBN 978-0-9978065-2-6
First Printing

This book is to honor:

the Christian example
Manfred and Christina Freissle
have given their family and the world,

our dear HWAW friend, Fernando Garcia,

and all the CEOs wanting
to honor God in their company.

TABLE OF CONTENTS

PETER FREISSLE

Peter Freissle is the President and CEO of Polydeck Screen Corporation; a company with approximately 300 employees in the US, Chile and Peru. Polydeck makes screens used in mining material such as coal, aggregate, precious stones and ores. Laser focused on creating a culture of "Care" within Polydeck, all company activities and processes are filtered through their Core Values of "humility, honesty, integrity, respect, kindness and a sense of social responsibility."

Almost 10 years ago Peter founded HWAW, a 501 c3, non for profit, with a mission to create eternal value in the workplace around the world by helping decision makers understand the importance of caring for people in a way that honors God; thereby generating EternalROI™, an eternal return on investment.

Peter is a proud father of four children, who are frequently by his side during community and charity support work with organizations like Chosen Children-Genesis Project, Hope Remains Ranch, Mobile Meals, Hope for Children, Habitat for Humanity and SPIHN of which he is the founding Board member. SPIHN offers homeless children and parents a way off the streets and a path to self-sufficiency.

In addition to the many cherished affiliations within the national and international workplace ministry movement, Peter has served for a number of years as an active member of the Board of Directors for Corporate Chaplains of America.

For more about Polydeck, please see the Polydeck Case Study included in the appendix.

FORWARD

From Peter Freissle
Founder of His Way at Work and subject of the Business Card Book

Since starting His Way at Work (HWAW) almost ten years ago, I have been blessed to have met and been inspired by many business owners that want to honor God through their company. Some have taken a few small steps and some have taken large steps, but many of them still want to learn more about how they can serve the Eternal purpose of the organization across the entire company — not just at the top. The Key objective behind HWAW is to help organizations answer the question of how to create Eternal Value. This is accomplished by creating intentional processes and employee engagement that leads to caring for people in a way that honors God, all the way from the CEO to the Janitor, with each person being seen not as a "Human Resource" but rather as a "Soul" that God has placed within the organization. As one CEO put it, "I see my role as enriching the lives of my employees with the gifts that God has blessed me with."

This guide is designed to help leaders who are ready to take the Leap of Faith with a process and a support group from other CEOs that have already jumped. Here are a few simple things to consider before starting your His Way at Work "Leap of Faith" journey:

1. Are you doing it to get something or are you doing it to give something in response to God's many gifts to you and His calling to… "Love one another. As I have loved you, so you must love one another" (John 13:34). This question points towards "Purity of Intention." As you begin your HWAW journey, you will discover many potential financial benefits that come from employee engagement, improved moral, reduction in employee turnover, improved productivity, etc. However, always remember, "Seek first his kingdom and his righteousness, and all these things will be given to you as well" (Matt. 6:33).

2. Ignatius of Loyola suggests that before we make such a major decision, we first prayerfully imagine ourselves at our deathbed and then ask what we would have wished we had chosen.

3. Have you spent time with the Lord to discern what the true purpose of your life is? It will help to write your Purpose Statement in one or two sentences as a guide for your future course of action. As Mark Twain said, "The two most important days of your life are the day you are born and the day you find out why."

4. What is the true purpose of the business that God has gifted to you? Does your business have a Purpose Statement? Have you considered the Eternal purpose of your business? As Jesus reminded His disciples "Do not store up for yourselves treasures on earth, where moths and vermin destroy, and where thieves break in and steal. But store up for yourselves treasures in heaven" (Matt. 6:19-20).

5. Will there be enough evidence of your Christian principles and values that everyone in your company will know what these principles are, that the company cares for them and the company is there to display the love of God in real and practical terms when they are in a crisis and need support?

A LEAP OF FAITH

Buck Jacobs mentions in his inspiring book "A Light shines bright in Babylon," we as business leaders have a Holy Calling to run the businesses God has gifted to us for His glory and for the building up and equipping of His Body. As you set about to answer this Holy Calling and fulfill the Eternal Purpose of your business, there are many fears that will confront you. These might include:

1. What will my Leadership Team think?
2. What will my employees think?
3. Will I lose customers?
4. How much will this cost me?
5. Will there be litigation?

Overcoming these fears will require you to take a "leap of faith," but rest assured that the Master of the Universe is right there with you and it is the desire of His heart to see you succeed. As you begin your journey, there are a few virtues that are important to consider.

Love:

After I returned from a retreat, I was on an emotional high. I felt this burning desire in my heart to share this feeling of God's love with everyone. But how would I do that? I thought back to stories and movies I had seen about the crusaders of the Middle Ages; they too had a burning desire to share their message with the world. As I reflected on this, it became clear to me that while their original intent was understandable, their execution was terrible; they were intent on declaring Christ, but did so without displaying His Love.

The lesson I learned from this was not to try to Bible bash anyone, but rather to create an environment in which the love of God is first demonstrated and then hope that there is enough evidence of God's love that people are attracted to the source of that love, God Himself, for God is LOVE. God does not force us to love Him, but rather gently calls each of us in the stillness of our hearts and loves us with that unconditional love. In the same way, we are called as business leaders to gently sow the seeds of the Gospel with love.

Respect:

One of the essential elements of this love is respect, especially in the workplace, where people of every faith and creed gather to work. We are called to share the Gospel while respecting others' faith or lack of faith. For at the end of the day we are called to sow the seeds and it is not by force, but rather by love and the gentle power of the Holy Spirit that these seeds will grow.

In order for people to believe in an invisible God, they seek visible signs of the existence of God and the fruits of His Love in the real world. It is, therefore, important to first exhibit an authentic desire to live the message through practical acts of caring, generosity, kindness, respect, and love in the workplace before you begin to share Christ. There is an old saying "Nobody cares how much you know until they know how much you care."

Humility:

However, it is essential that as leaders, your actions and communications are done with humility, as there will be times when we, as all humans do (I can personally testify to this), will fail to live an authentic Christian example. So it is not as important to live a perfect life as it is to demonstrate your willingness to strive for perfection and ask for forgiveness when we fail. As Mother Teresa said, "We are merely pencils in God's hands."

Patience:

One of the best pieces of advice I received early on was to be patient. Like many Type-A CEOs, I wanted to put my caring programs into high gear, but I learned that trying to tackle too many caring programs at one time can lead to disaster. So my advice is to start slowly with one or two projects and do them with excellence and allow the positive momentum to move from there: "slow and steady wins the race." Or, as Mother Teresa once said, "We can do no great things, only small things with great love."

Prayer:

Everything starts with prayer. On this journey, there are many stumbling blocks, obstacles and even the temptation to quit. Daily prayer is the nourishment that sustains us and allows the Holy Spirit to fill our hearts with the fire of God's love.

> *"Love is patient, love is kind. It does not envy, it does not boast, it is not proud. It does not dishonor others, it is not self-seeking, it is not easily angered, it keeps no record of wrongs. Love does not delight in evil but rejoices with the truth. It always protects, always trusts, always hopes, always perseveres. Love never fails."*
>
> 1 Corinthians 13:4–8

Let me conclude with three simple quotes by Francis of Assisi:

> *"It is no use walking anywhere to preach unless our walking is our preaching."*
>
> *"Preach the Gospel always, and when absolutely necessary, use words."*
>
> *"All the darkness in the world cannot extinguish the light of a single candle."*

May the Lord fill your heart with His Love and light your candle with the fire of His love so that it may shine brightly to enable others to find their way closer to God, our loving Father who wishes to welcome all His children into their Heavenly home. The words, thoughts and ideas contained in this book are a collection of many experiences that God has blessed us with and we take no credit for them, they are offered to you as encouragement along your journey in the workplace ministry movement and are intended for one purpose only, to give all praise and glory to our Lord Jesus. May God bless you on your journey and remember, we are all in this together and your participation is paramount.

Ready to jump?

WHY THE TRANSFORMATION GUIDE?

We are pleased to add the Transformation Guide to our current offering. We hope it will complement our coaching and membership services to help facilitate our mission by offering you a more direct path to developing Eternal value within your company.

The purpose of this guide is to offer an accessible, affordable way to introduce you and your company to the His Way at Work model in a format that allows you to implement caring initiatives using your internal resources. To fully utilize this guide, we invite you to spend time in the chapter prayers, take the assessments, work through each step with discernment and use our templates and resources available through the web link on the last page of the book. To make the most of your experience with His Way at Work, we recommend that you use this guide as a complement to our other services.

TOOLS TO HELP YOU CREATE ETERNAL VALUE		
The Transformation Guide	*Membership*	*Coaching*
• An introductory guide to HWAW • Structured step by step tool • Self paced implementation option	• Connects CEO's and Caring Leaders • Shares best practices and company examples • Provides materials and tools for learning	• Trained coaches • Virtual coaches • Hands on coaching

There are 3 options for using the Transformation Guide depending on your company needs.

HOW TO USE THE TRANSFORMATION GUIDE			
	Option 1	Option 2	Option 3
Transformation Guide	✓	✓	✓
Membership		✓	✓
Coaching			✓

Option 1 *is for companies that:*
- Are not sure if they are ready for the journey and want to learn more
- Want to try on their own first

Option 2 *is for companies that:*
- Have limited funds
- Have strong internal resources qualified and available to lead the implementation and/or serve as the Caring Facilitator or Mission Officer
- Want to develop and connect their Caring Leaders or Mission Officers with other Caring Leaders and Mission Officers
- Want to develop and connect with other CEO's
- Want to share successes and failures with HWAW and across companies

Option 3 *is for companies that:*
- Want to move faster by using the expertise of a trained coach
- Do not have a strong internal resource available to lead the implementation or serve as a Caring Leader or Mission Officer
- Want to develop and connect their Caring Leaders or Mission Officers with other Caring Leaders and Mission Officers
- Want to develop and connect with other CEO's
- Want to share successes and failures

Thank you for purchasing the guide and we hope you will find it helpful on your journey to create Eternal Value! If you have any questions, please contact us as *hwaw.com*. Examples, templates and testimonies referenced in the guide are available at *hwaw.com/guideresources*. Please log in and register to access.

HIS WAY AT WORK
What Matters Most

We hope this guide will help YOU on your journey to transform your company's culture with the Light of Christ!

Sincerely,

The His Way at Work Team

Peter Freissle
Founder and President of Polydeck

Scott Gajewsky
Caring and Culture Manager for Polydeck

Alfonso Gonzalez
Board Member, Founder and Chairman of Qualfon

William Renfrow
Founding Board Member, CEO of Renfrow Brothers

Martin Tighe
Board Member, CEO and Founder of Donnelly Communications

Roberto Mejorada Sanchez
Board Member, Chief Mission Officer of Qualfon

Armando Del Bosque
Executive Director

Kelly Slate
Operations and Learning Director

Regional HWAW Coaches
Visit hwaw.com for the coach directory

It Starts With

A CEO AND
A PURPOSE

1

In January 2013, in Cancun, Mexico, Peter was preparing to share his story at the first annual HWAW event. As he does before meeting with business leaders, he asked God, "Will anyone show up? Am I worthy to do this? Please help me to say the right things for You; please speak through me; please help us to accomplish our mission to inspire and educate CEOs to improve their workplace by having God at the center and caring for people as He did, to create Eternal Value."

After Peter finished his talk to over 100 CEOs, one man immediately moved toward him with excitement and great emotion. This man was the CEO of a large, multinational hotel chain. He has been a faithful Christian his entire life. He raised his children in the church, attends church faithfully, gives to the community, spends time in Bible studies with local businessmen, and has a reputation of genuinely caring for people like Jesus did, but he did not know how to declare and display this love at work. He looked at Peter with tears of joy in his eyes and said, *"I finally get it Peter, my purpose as a CEO is to help bring my employees to heaven."*

◆ ◆ ◆

The HWAW Transformation starts with a CEO and a Purpose. Not just any CEO. Not just any purpose.

◆ ◆ ◆

The HWAW CEO understands that his leadership in his company is a gift, it is stewardship, it is servanthood; it is temporary and how he leads has eternal implications. He knows he is accountable to God for how he runs his company, the culture he creates and how he invests his profits. He is ready to respond to God's call and is now looking for help on how to best do this from other CEOs that have accepted the same call.

The HWAW CEO must be willing to make five commitments in order to truly transform the culture of his company:

The first commitment

You are willing to first display, then declare, your love for God to employees, their families, clients, vendors, and communities.

The second commitment

You are willing to maintain the daily habits of prayer, discernment, reading the Word and living your Christian Core Values to continue to strengthen your relationship with God.

The third commitment

You are willing to manage caring like a strategic initiative and will provide the resources required to support it.

The fourth commitment

You are willing to help cascade engagement by giving the decision making about how to best care for employees, employees' families, and the community to the employees.

The fifth commitment

You are willing to integrate your Caring Strategy into the organization so that it can continue to exist in a sustainable way even when you are no longer the leader.

◆ ◆ ◆

A HWAW CEO knows that God provides the products, people and profits that make a business, but these are not the end. These are merely a vehicle, a means to an end. The end is to create **Eternal Value** for the King of our hearts. Eternal Value refers to the things in life that will remain valuable forever, such as your relationship with God and the people you reach through caring and sharing like Jesus taught us. The ultimate purpose of a HWAW company is to honor God by providing ways to create Eternal Value. A HWAW CEO not only asks, "how do we make a profit," but is always asking, "how are we using profit to create Eternal Value?" just as, someday, God will ask each of us, "how did you use the gifts I gave you?"

By using the gifts God has given you as the CEO, you can provide a Caring Company Culture with the ultimate God-honoring purpose of creating Eternal Value.

If you are not a CEO, but want to honor God in your workplace, we welcome you to read this guide and see how you can apply it within your sphere of influence.

> *"Business is a meaningful and worthwhile endeavor that is self-funding and allows us to achieve our entire purpose for God."*
> — HWAW CEO

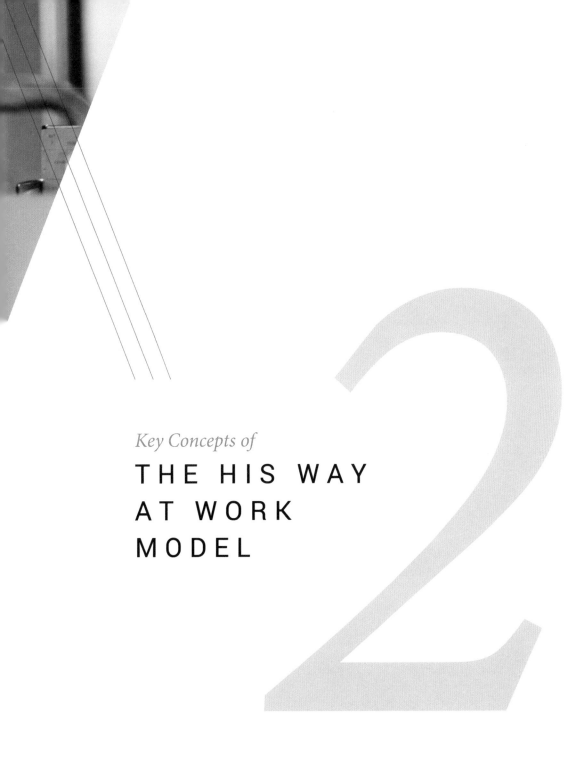

Key Concepts of

THE HIS WAY AT WORK MODEL

LEADER'S PRAYER

Dear Lord,

I thank You for opening my heart to want to find ways to create Eternal Value in our company for You. Thank You for bringing me this far on this journey. Please continue to walk with me as I learn more about the HWAW process and begin to think about how I can use it to implement a caring culture in our company.

> *"I desire to do your will, my God; your law is within my heart."*
> PSALM 40:8

Please help me to remember that I am not alone and I can turn to You any time for discernment and prayer and that HWAW is always here to help me as well. In the end all of the success on this journey is for You.

In Your Name,
Amen

Our Purpose:

To Create Eternal Value

Our Mission:

To inspire and help business leaders to improve their workplaces by having God at the center and caring for people as He did

Our Core Values:

To serve with love, faith and respect

Our Model:

The His Way at Work model is based on the following biblical principles:

1. Create Eternal Value.
2. Love your employees, their families, and your community like your neighbors.
3. Do this with excellence.
4. Do this with respect.

The HWAW methodology was designed by incorporating these beliefs into a best practice business model that can be implemented and replicated as the leadership commits to the ultimate God-honoring purpose of providing Eternal Value. We use the following concepts to communicate how we integrate these principles into the workplace.

> *"Each of you should use whatever gift you have received to serve others, as faithful stewards of God's grace in its various forms."*
> 1 PETER 4:10

HWAW CONCEPT #1
Create Eternal Return on Investment Through a Caring Company Culture

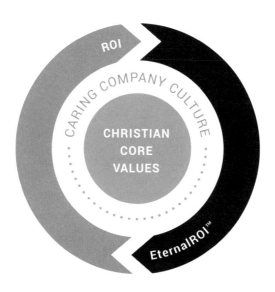

Organizational Culture

> *"We either: control and shape it or it controls and shapes us."*
> — HWAW

Company culture refers to the beliefs, core values, and behaviors that guide how all levels of a company's employees interact in all aspects of the business. This includes interactions both internal and external. If you do not shape the culture by providing the purpose, core values and behaviors expected by the company, then it will shape itself organically over time based on the core values and behaviors from the existing management or from the employees that are hired over time.

The company culture, whether on purpose or by accident, will be present in the day-to-day actions and decisions, including how employees treat each other, clients and vendor relationships, benefits, hiring profiles, business hours, and turnover. If not managed intentionally, a company's culture will become incompatible with its core values and beliefs.

A Caring Company Culture begins by living with Christian Core Values that promote genuine caring for employees, their families, and the communities where they live and work, including customers, vendors and suppliers through caring activities. As genuine caring is demonstrated, Eternal Value (EternalROI™) is created and thus morale, engagement and productivity grow. These also lead to increased profits as a byproduct, which is, in turn, re-invested in Caring Activities, thus creating a virtuous cycle of ROI–EternalROI™.

What is EternalROI™?

Many companies have a purpose to earn money, therefore focusing on ROI only. Some companies have a purpose to earn money and care for their employees physically and emotionally (or intellectually), therefore focusing on ROI and some caring. However, this caring may have the intentions to keep people happy so they can make more money for the company or to meet social responsibility obligations.

HWAW companies have a purpose to honor God, therefore focusing on ROI to provide the funds to care for people in a way that honors God with the ultimate goal of providing EternalROI™.

EternalROI™ are those activities in a company that are in place for the 'soul' purpose to create Eternal Value, therefore honoring God. These include Caring Leaders and Activities that may allow employees to either learn about Christ through the caring or develop a stronger relationship through the caring. This can be done through physical, emotional and spiritual Caring Activities but they should be done to serve the ultimate purpose, not ROI or ROI and caring.

Doing this, we honor God. Every time we care for someone, we lay the ground for "pay it forward" caring to take place. We preach with our actions, prompting others to do the same in an endless (Eternal) virtuous cycle.

> *"God bestows more consideration on the purity of intention with which our actions are performed than on the actions themselves."*
> — AUGUSTINE OF HIPPO

What does a Caring Company Culture founded on Christian values look like?

Since the ultimate goal is to create a Caring Company Culture that can provide EternalROI™, we should explain what this looks like inside the company. Here are a few examples (which may be culturally dependent):

1. Employees at all levels genuinely care for each other through daily actions.
2. Employees are aware of the needs of each other.
3. Employees are motivated, engaged and willing to go above and beyond for the company because they know the company will do the same for them.
4. Employees openly demonstrate the company's Core Values through their behaviors because they are aware of them, they align with their own and they want to live them even if they were not asked.
5. Purpose and Core Values are a common language.
6. Teams welcome prayer together even if they are not Christian.
7. Teams want to pray for each other even if they are not Christian.
8. Team members are there when you need them.
9. When you want to learn something new or change paths, you have support to do so.
10. When you mess up, you are forgiven.
11. Excellence is expected.
12. When terminations are required, the person is treated with dignity.
13. People want to work for this company.
14. People don't want to leave the company unless it is for personal reasons or other opportunities for growth.
15. When people leave for personal reasons or opportunities for growth, they are supported and encouraged.
16. Employees care for each other even when the boss is out.
17. Employees say yes to overtime not for the money, but to help the company.
18. Employees are willing to sacrifice pay in the bad times to help the company.
19. Employees look for ways to be good stewards for the company.
20. There is an environment of trust because everyone is focused on the same purpose, not individual needs.
21. There is healthy focus on safety within the company and for each other.

HWAW KEY CONCEPT #2
How We Love Our Employees, Their Families and the Community Like Our Neighbors

THE CARING MATRIX:

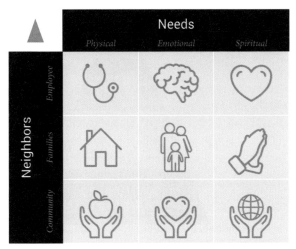

"Love the Lord your God with all your heart and with all your soul and with all your mind.' This is the first and greatest commandment. And the second is like it: 'Love your neighbor as yourself.'"

MATTHEW 22:37–39

One way to love the invisible God is to love the visible neighbors that are around us all the time in the workplace. By caring for your employees and their families as well as caring for the communities in which they live and work, you are, in effect, loving your neighbor.

The Caring Matrix is our unique tool for helping companies love their employees, families, and community like their neighbors by providing Caring Activities to not only meet physical and emotional needs, but also, most importantly: spiritual needs. Through living with Christian Core Values and providing Caring Activities, employees are able to demonstrate genuine caring for each other like the neighbors they are.

A Caring Team comprised of employees across the company uses the Caring Matrix as their key tool for ensuring Caring Activities are in place for employees, their families, and the community to meet physical, emotional, and spiritual needs. The Caring Team is the way for the company to promote engagement in the HWAW process throughout the organization.

HWAW 4 STEP PROCESS

Align the Vision Team

Create Your Implementation Plan

Cascade Engagement

Live Out His Way at Work

CEO

VISION TEAM

CARING TEAM

COMMUNITIES, FAMILIES, & EMPLOYEES

As HWAW is sharing testimonies from HWAW CEOs and Companies, we are often asked to help others replicate the transformation process. Although we believe the transformation is unique for each company and is guided by the grace of God, based on our experience working with many companies, we believe the same basic steps will apply for all transformations. We integrated the activities that have proven to work so far with over 70 companies into a 4-step process. This process can be used regardless of where you are starting from on your journey while still allowing the who, what, how, and when to be customized to fit the needs of the company.

Where you are in this journey will determine the specific steps you will need to take. By following these steps, we can help you find out where and how to begin. We can help speed up your transformation process by minimizing or eliminating potential pitfalls inherent in doing something for the first time and/or in a non-systematic way.

We can also provide a method to measure, sustain, and continually improve your company's caring results.

HWAW KEY CONCEPT #4
How We Do This With Respect

> *"There is only one God and he is God to all; therefore it is important that everyone is seen as equal before God. I've always said we should help a Hindu become a better Hindu, a Muslim become a better Muslim, a Catholic become a better Catholic. We believe our work should be our example to people."*
>
> — MOTHER TERESA

The most frequently asked question from CEOs that believe and want to be "all in" is how we do this in a way that does not offend those that do not believe or do believe but do not feel there is a place for faith in the workplace. The answer is simple: "We do this with respect."

We must demonstrate genuine care first before we are able to share why we are caring.

> *"But in your hearts revere Christ as Lord. Always be prepared to give an answer to everyone who asks you to give the reason for the hope that you have. But do this with gentleness and respect."*
>
> 1 PETER 3:15-16

HWAW is a biblical Christian organization who serves all faiths equally. We have learned that the majority of faiths, Christian or not, have an element of caring for each other and share a common Golden Rule. The Golden Rule is referred to in the teaching of these various faiths. By referring to what we share and have in common, we are able to understand what caring for each other looks like without being offensive, discriminatory or creating fear.

In many of our initial workshops with CEOs and their Leadership Teams, this subject emerges from the discussion. Whether the question is raised by a Christian that is not comfortable bringing their faith into the work place or by a non-Christian that is not comfortable being asked to participate, it will come out eventually. We believe you should encourage the conversation. Get it out in the open to discuss so you at least have the opportunity to have an open conversation that demonstrates respect and the Golden Rule. We will share more on this topic in the next chapter.

NOTES

THE HIS
WAY AT WORK
ASSESSMENTS

Planning the Way Forward

PURPOSE:

To help the Transformation Leader understand where they are today in the journey as a leader, a member of the Leadership Team, and as an organization.

LEADER'S PRAYER

Dear Lord,

Thank You for being with me on this journey. I am so grateful for Your love and mercy. As I begin to review the assessments in this chapter, please help me answer with humility and truth. Help me look in the mirror with an open heart and mind so I can truly understand where I am and where the organization is on this journey. Help me see where we need to go and give me the strength and courage to get there so we can achieve our purpose of honoring You.

> *"For by the grace given me I say to every one of you:*
> *Do not think of yourself more highly than you ought,*
> *but rather think of yourself with sober judgment, in*
> *accordance with the faith God has distributed to each*
> *of you."*
> ROMANS 12:3

Please help me to remember that I am not in this alone and I can turn to You at any time for discernment and prayer and that HWAW is here for me also. In the end, all of the success from this journey is for YOU.

In Your Name,
Amen

We started working with a health services provider where most employees worked in different locations across the region. The CEO was a very strong and faithful Christian. She was active in the Church, a member of many Christian business organizations and gave to her community. She heard Peter speak at a conference in early 2014.

After this, she went back to work. She added 'to honor God' in her mission statement and began implementing a couple Caring Activities, including a corporate chaplain, a place to pray, and a small recognition program of giving gift cards. Still, she felt like she was not doing enough. As much as she tried to make changes to the culture, she felt her Leadership Team was not engaged and she was trying to sustain these changes on her own. She asked HWAW for help.

◆ ◆ ◆

What are the HWAW Assessments?

We recommend starting with three assessments:

1. The HWAW Leader Self-Assessment
2. The HWAW Organization Assessment
3. The Table Group's 5 Dysfunctions of a Team Assessment

HWAW Leader Assessment

The HWAW Leader Assessment is a tool to help the leader validate where he is on his own journey to honor God and put Him at the center of his life as a person and as a leader, sharing his experience with employees, customers, suppliers, family, and society in general, in and out of work. This assessment helps him to think about how he is living his faith in an integrated way with his life at home, at work, and in the community — not just at church. Is he living it with all his being, with all his thoughts, his words, his actions, his activities, his desires, his intentions and his behaviors, in and out of work, with openness, with respect, knowledge, wisdom, commitment, coherence, confidence, and love? Or is he living his faith ashamed, afraid and insecure, according to his own interests and priorities? We recommend that this survey be administered to the CEO for his personal review and reflection as he starts the HWAW process.

HWAW Organization Assessment

The HWAW Organization Assessment is a tool to help the leader and the Leadership Team understand where they are on this journey as a team and as a company and what they need to focus on as they develop the implementation plan. The results of this assessment identify the current strengths and gaps based on the opinion of the leader and team and helps target the areas to celebrate and the areas to work on in the implementation plan.

Table Group's 5 Dysfunctions of a Team Assessment

The Table Group's 5 Dysfunctions of a Team Assessment provides your executive team with a sense of its strengths and areas for improvement. While the Assessment itself is certainly quantitative and data-driven, its most important aspect is the qualitative perspective it provides for your team and the discussion that it provokes around specific issues. This assessment can also be used for the Caring Team once it is in place. This assessment is available at *tablegroup.com* for a fee. The Table Group also offers an Organization Health Assessment for free at *tablegroup.com*.

Why should I complete these assessments?

HWAW Leader Assessment

Through this Assessment, we can accompany the leader in his journey in a respectful manner that is firm, open and loving. We can decide on common goals for the consistent practice of the transcendent purpose of the company through the practice of values and Christian virtues.

HWAW Organization Assessment

It is difficult to develop a plan if you do not have an objective view of where you are today.

5 Dysfunctions of a Team Assessment

Striving to create a functional, cohesive team is one of the few remaining competitive advantages available to any organization looking for a powerful point of differentiation. Functional teams get more accomplished in less time than other teams because they avoid wasting time on the wrong issues and revisiting the same topics again and again. They also make higher quality decisions and stick to those decisions by eliminating politics and confusion among themselves and the people they lead.

Finally, functional teams keep their best employees longer because "A" players rarely leave organizations where they are part of, or being led by, a cohesive team. To learn more about this assessment, visit *tablegroup.com*.

ASSESSMENT 1

HWAW Leader Self-Assessment	Always 5	Often 4	Some 3	Seldom 2	Never 1
Leader's Personal Beliefs					
I believe in and accept Jesus Christ as my Lord and Savior.	☐	☐	☐	☐	☐
I love God with all my heart, soul and mind.	☐	☐	☐	☐	☐
I love my neighbor as myself.	☐	☐	☐	☐	☐
I pray daily and seek God's wisdom and direction in all that I do.	☐	☐	☐	☐	☐
I encourage others to develop a personal relationship with God.	☐	☐	☐	☐	☐
I help disciple those seeking to grow in their faith.	☐	☐	☐	☐	☐
Leader's Business Beliefs					
I believe God owns my company in which I am just a servant and a steward of what He has entrusted to me.	☐	☐	☐	☐	☐
I am committed to running my business on Christian principles.	☐	☐	☐	☐	☐
I want the employees to love and respect one another.	☐	☐	☐	☐	☐
I want the company to serve all faiths equally, coming from a biblical Christian frame of reference.	☐	☐	☐	☐	☐
I strive to operate the company with excellence to glorify God and profitably to fund its Purpose.	☐	☐	☐	☐	☐
I operate the business in ethical ways and with integrity.	☐	☐	☐	☐	☐
Leader's Style and Tone					
My words, attitudes and actions reflect to everyone my desire to conduct business according to Christian values and principles.	☐	☐	☐	☐	☐
I ensure that all employees know I am accessible through my "Open Door Policy."	☐	☐	☐	☐	☐
I display Christ's love through my actions, showing appreciation and respect for all my employees and business contacts.	☐	☐	☐	☐	☐
I promote and encourage development and growth by bringing out the best in others.	☐	☐	☐	☐	☐
I reflect a "servant leader" style of leadership as modeled by Jesus.	☐	☐	☐	☐	☐
I am open to humbly receive constructive criticism from all employees.	☐	☐	☐	☐	☐
I have implemented an anonymous employee survey to receive feedback from all employees.	☐	☐	☐	☐	☐
I lead voluntary prayer during meetings and events.	☐	☐	☐	☐	☐

ASSESSMENT 2

HWAW Organization Assessment	Always 5	Often 4	Some 3	Seldom 2	Never 1
Organization's Strategy, Structure and Core Values					
The business is performed with excellence in all areas.	☐	☐	☐	☐	☐
The company has a purpose statement reflecting "why" it exists.	☐	☐	☐	☐	☐
The purpose statement is available to all employees.	☐	☐	☐	☐	☐
The business is used as a mission field with our "bottom line profit" seen as a gift from God to be used to create eternal value.	☐	☐	☐	☐	☐
A mission statement is in place stating "what" the organization desires to accomplish.	☐	☐	☐	☐	☐
The mission statement is shared with employees.	☐	☐	☐	☐	☐
The mission statement is being lived out by the organization.	☐	☐	☐	☐	☐
A Core Values statement has been developed stating "how" the organization will behave.	☐	☐	☐	☐	☐
The Core Values statement is grounded in Christian principles.	☐	☐	☐	☐	☐
The Core Values statement is available to all employees.	☐	☐	☐	☐	☐
All employees are held accountable to these values.	☐	☐	☐	☐	☐
The Core Values of the company are "lived out" through a Caring Plan.	☐	☐	☐	☐	☐
Organization's Caring Strategy					
The Caring Plan is incorporated into the company's business plan (including the company's metrics or KPI's).	☐	☐	☐	☐	☐
A Caring Team (a cross-functional, employee-led committee) carries out the organization's Caring Plan.	☐	☐	☐	☐	☐
The Caring Team solicits recommendations and ideas from all employees.	☐	☐	☐	☐	☐
Multiple communication channels are in place to share/celebrate the organization's Caring Plan with all employees and their families.	☐	☐	☐	☐	☐
A percentage of sales or profits are set aside to fund the organization's Caring Plan.	☐	☐	☐	☐	☐
A program to allow employees to recognize fellow employees who exhibit the core value behaviors is in place ("Caught You Caring").	☐	☐	☐	☐	☐

ASSESSMENT 3

Team Health Assessment

HWAW has found the stronger the organizational health of the Leadership Team, the higher chance there is of HWAW implementation being successful. We will discuss this more in Step 1, Aligning Your Leadership Team, but if you have any doubts on the health of your team, we recommend that your Leadership Team refer to the books and tools that can be found on their website at tablegroup.com. HWAW offers a trained coach for *The 5 Dysfunctions of a Team* that can help you as well.

How to complete these Assessments?

Assessment 1and 2:

Go to *hwaw.com/self-assessment/* or *hwaw.com/organization-assessment/* to register for the on-line survey. Once the on-line survey is completed, we will provide you with the following:

1. Your survey results.
2. A Gap Assessment that indicates areas where you are strong or have opportunities to strengthen.
3. A recommendation to pay attention to specific HWAW Process steps where you need to focus your time.

Assessment #3:

Go to *tablegroup.com* to purchase the team assessment or use the free organizational health assessment.

COMPANY RESULTS

Results from Assessment #2

Self Assessment Gap Analysis Questions	CEO	Leadership Team Average	CEO and Leadership Team Average	GAP	GAP%
The business is performed with excellence in all areas.	4.0	3.3	3.3	0.7	-18%
The company has a purpose statement reflecting why it exists.	5.0	3.9	3.9	1.1	-22%
The purpose statement is available to all employees.	1.0	3.3	3.3	2.3	233%
The business is used as a mission field with our "bottom line profit" seen as a gift from God to be used to create eternal value.	5.0	4.5	4.5	0.5	-10%
A mission statement is in place stating "what" the organization desires to accomplish.	5.0	4.4	4.4	0.6	-12%
The mission statement is shared with employees.	5.0	4.4	4.4	0.6	-12%
The organization is living out the mission statement.	5.0	4.2	4.2	0.6	-16%
A Core Values statement has been developed stating "how" the organization will behave.	5.0	4.3	4.3	0.7	-14%
The Core Values statement is grounded in Christian principles.	5.0	4.9	4.9	0.1	-2%
The Core Values statement is available to all employees.	5.0	4.2	4.2	0.8	-16%
All employees are held accountable to these values.	3.0	3.1	3.1	0.1	3%
The Core Values of the company are "lived out" through a Caring Plan.	2.0	2.8	2.8	0.8	40%
The Caring Plan is incorporated into the company's business plan (including company's metrics or KPI's).	2.0	2.0	2.0	0.0	0%
A Caring Team (a cross-functional, employee-led committee) carries out the organization's Caring Plan.	1.0	1.8	1.8	0.8	80%
The Caring Team solicits recommendations and ideas from all employees.	1.0	2.1	2.1	1.1	110%
Multiple communication channels are in place to share/celebrate the organization's Caring Plan with all employees and their families.	1.0	2.0	2.0	1.0	100%
A percentage of sales or profits are set aside to fund the organization's Caring Plan.	1.0	2.3	2.3	1.3	130%
A program to allow employees to recognize fellow employees who exhibit the core value behaviors is in place ("Caught You Caring").	1.0	2.5	2.5	1.5	150%

Results from Assessment #3

5 Dysfunctions of a Team Survey

	Never 1	Seldom 2	Some 3	Often 4	Always 5

Results ━━━━━━━━━━ *3.77%*

Your score in this area was high, which indicates that your team values collective outcomes more than individual recognition and attainment of status.

Accountability ━━━━━━━━ *3.43%*

Your score in this area was medium, which indicates that your team may be hesitating to confront one another about performance and behavioral concerns.

Commitment ━━━━━━━━ *3.65%*

Your score in this area was medium, which indicates that your team may struggle at times to buy-in to clear decisions. This could be creating ambiguity within the organization.

Conflict ━━━━━━━━ *3.53%*

Your score in this area was medium, which indicates that your team may need to learn to engage in more unfiltered discussion around important topics.

Trust ━━━━━━━━ *3.70%*

Your score in this area was medium, which indicates that your team may need to get more comfortable being vulnerable and open with one another about individual strengths, weaknesses, mistakes and needs for help.

Your overall scores indicate that "Results" is a likely area of strength for your team, while the other categories are potentially areas for improvement.

The results indicated the following:

Strengths:

- The Leader is ready to jump (meets the 5 commitments to implement HWAW)
- The Leader has support in place to help implement changes
- Some caring is in place already (chaplain, chapel, gift cards, heart of the leader)
- The leader is willing to spend ROI to generate EternalROI™

Opportunities:

- The mission is the Leader's mission — the Leadership Team is not aligned or engaged
- The organization has linked Core Values to behaviors but has not integrated them with HR practices
- There is no Caring Strategy, just random programs
- The Caring Strategy is not being treated like a strategic initiative — just a side project of the leader
- The caring has not been cascaded to all employees
- There are no metrics or action plans for improvement
- There is no communication plan
- The Leadership Team needs some team development around trust, conflict, commitment, and accountability

Even though the Leader is "all-in" and has implemented some important Caring Activities, we recommend that we go through all the steps to ensure we have the foundations in place for a sustainable change in our company culture. In the end, our mission is not just to talk about creating Eternal value, but to help business leaders to improve their workplace by having God at the center and caring for people as He did.

Recap

Before going to the next step, we encourage you to go to *hwaw.com/organization-assessment/* and take our assessment. Next, take some time to write down the key learnings from your assessment results.

What does your assessment say?

_____

_____

_____

What are your key strengths?

_____

_____

_____

What are your key gaps?

_____

_____

What areas are you committing to work on?

_____

_____

How are you going to hold yourself accountable to this step?

_____

_____

NOTES

STEP ONE

Aligning the Vision Team

PURPOSE:

Initial formal introduction to the Vision Team of
where the CEO wants to go, why, and how to get there.

LEADER'S PRAYER

Dear Lord,

I know as a member of our Leadership Team, I am responsible for being a good steward and servant and I am accountable to You for the company and people I lead. As I move into the next step of sharing this journey with my Leadership Team, please help me lead with You by my side and in my heart. Help me be transparent as I share my own journey, help me have the courage to keep moving forward when faced with opposition and help me to remember the Key Concept #4 of respect when working with others that may not understand why providing Eternal Value is the MOST important in our life on earth.

I am aware of the Spiritual Warfare that will take place as I move on this journey, closer and closer to serving Your purpose. I know there will be difficult times that may involve deep suffering for myself, my family, and my Leadership Team so please give us strength and perseverance. I also know that I can stay the course as long as I keep You in the forefront of every step I take.

> *"With man this is impossible, but not with God; all things are possible with God."*
> MARK 10:27

Please help me to remember that I am not in this alone and I can turn to You at any time for discernment and prayer and that HWAW is here for me also. In the end, all of the success from this journey is for YOU.

In Your Name,
Amen

1 *Align the Vision Team*

2 *Create Your Implementation Plan*

3 *Cascade Engagement*

4 *Live Out His Way at Work*

We arrived for the initial meeting with a CEO and his Leadership Team. At this point, the CEO is fully aware of the HWAW model, the assessment results and our recommended path forward for his team and the organization. The objective of this meeting is to align the Leadership Team. This Leadership Team knows the CEO is a Christian who wants to do more, has heard of HWAW and seen some of the changes he has made, but does not know the model and the expectations for moving forward. From what we have learned so far, we know this team has some BIG fears and some big ROI pressures.

These fears may include not being confident in being able to hire and retain employees under these standards; acceptability from the board and customers; tension and frustration caused among employees in reaction to a new initiative; taking on more responsibilities when they don't always meet their already stated goals. What, the Leadership Team might wonder, is the CEO thinking?

◆ ◆ ◆

What is Step 1?

Step 1 is the initial formal introduction to the Leadership Team of where the CEO wants to go, why, and how to get there at a summary level. This step includes time to discuss potential fears within the Leadership Team and what will be expected from them as the company starts this journey.

Why should I complete Step 1?

It is very difficult to transform a company's culture if the Leadership Team is not aligned. They do not all have to believe in God and agree 100%, but they should be aligned and willing to hold hands before going to Step 2. The Leadership Team has to set this standard together and if they are not ready, we recommend to stop the process and spend time with the Leadership Team. *The Advantage* is a great resource.

How do I complete Step 1?

We recommend scheduling dedicated time for the CEO and Leadership Team to cover Chapters 4 and 5. This can be covered during an offsite meeting over 1–2 days or during several 1–2 hours sessions spread out over time. The amount of time will depend on where you are on your journey, the size of your organization, and the industry in which you work.

We encourage the CEO to include the Leadership Team during this process in an effort to model and improve the effectiveness of cascading engagement (Chapter 6). However, based on the style of the CEO or the size of the company, there will be situations where the CEO will start this process alone or with only one or two people comprising the Leadership Team. If you would like help from HWAW, please contact us at *hwaw.com*.

STEP 1 PROCESS

1.1 Share the Key Concepts with the Leadership Team

For the purpose of this guide, we define the Leadership Team as the core team responsible for helping the CEO to shape the company culture. If this group is different than the current Leadership Team, some companies refer to them as the Mission or Vision Team. For the purpose of this guide, we will refer to this group as the Vision Team.

The Vision Team is comprised of some, if not all, members of the executive Leadership Team that report directly to the CEO. They are the key decision makers involved in setting the budget, meeting the ROI targets and influencing the culture. We recommend that the Human Resources leader be included on this team.

Although we recommend (as a best practice), including the team in the decisions made in order to promote buy-in and speed of implementation, it does not mean the team must approve every decision. The CEO may have some 'non-negotiables' that do not require 100% buy-in from the team. For example, a CEO may choose to include the word "God" in the mission statement or Core Values even though the entire Vision Team has not bought into this idea. If you do not have 100% agreement, you do want 100% to agree to support it.

According to Patrick Lencioni in The 5 Dysfunctions of a Team, "a team is a relatively small number of people (anywhere from 3–13) that shares common goals as well as rewards and responsibilities for achieving them."

If the executive team is small (less than 13), we recommend including the entire team as the Vision Team. This will facilitate the buy-in process and ensure your Vision Team is sharing the same message about this initiative. If the executive team is greater than 13, we recommend you select from the group those that have the most influence on the organization. Vision Teams usually range from 4–8 in our HWAW coached companies.

Note: If the team directly reporting to the CEO is much larger than 13 then this could be an opportunity for the CEO to improve Organization Health. Refer to Discipline 1: Building a Cohesive team in *The Advantage* by Patrick Lencioni.

EXAMPLES OF VISION TEAMS

Company A:

Small Manufacturing Company, CEO Led, Less than 50 Employees, 2 locations

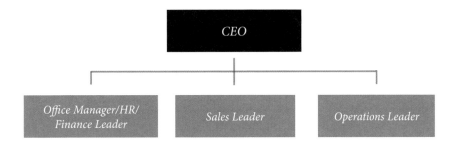

Company B: *Small Health Services Company, Partner Led, Less than 50 Employees*

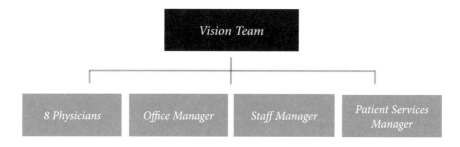

Company C: *Large Manufacturing Company, CEO Led, 14 Locations, 1200 Employees*

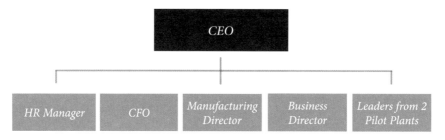

Company D: *Large Global Services Company, Founder Led, Over 15,000 Employees*

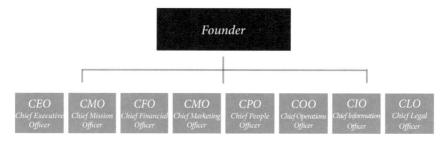

Next steps:
- Share Your Story with the Vision Team
  - ▷ Where are you on this journey?
  - ▷ Where do you want to go?
  - ▷ What is HWAW and how does it fit in your journey?
- Review HWAW Concepts with the Vision Team (Chap. 2)
- Conduct assessments with the Vision Team and review results (Chap. 3)

1.2 Overcome Four Potential Fears

There are at least 4 potential fears that may be stirring in the heads and hearts of the CEO and Vision Team members, even if they are 'all in' and ready to transform. We recommend getting these out on the table and working through them before moving to the next step. These fears are not in any particular order as in different cultures, countries, industries, and settings their relative weight may shift from one to another.

Fear #1: Will I Get Sued?

Particularly in a legalistic culture, we are frequently reminded by the news media of just how many legal battles take place each day, how complex the legal landscape is, and how costly the penalties can be. All of this is intimidating, especially to someone who is vested with protecting the interests of a business. The fear is that you would be risking it all by communicating your religious beliefs in the marketplace. The good news is that an employer is legally permitted to have a religious witness to the general public as well as to the company employees, and many do.

However there are several fairly simple legal principles and guidelines that must be followed in order to do it legally.

Business owners are permitted to communicate their religious beliefs through their company policies and practices so long as they do not give prospective or current employees the perception that employment or advancement in the company requires an employee to adopt the religious beliefs of the employer. In addition, the objections of the employees of other or no faiths must be accommodated and the employer may not mandate participation in religious worship.

It is not very difficult to stay on the right side of the law by applying some common sense and lots of sensitivity, compassion, and respect for the viewpoints and beliefs of others.

The following are suggested guidelines to consider when promoting employee participation in faith based events:

1. Participation in prayer and expressions of faith must be completely voluntary.
2. Employers must allow expressions of faith from different perspectives, religions, and religious points of view without fear or ridicule, harassment or reprisal.
3. Participation in events involving prayer and faith should not benefit any aspect of the employment of the participating employee.
4. If an employee chooses not to participate in events involving the expression of prayer and faith, they must not be disadvantaged in any way as it relates to their employment.

These guidelines are not intended to provide legal advice or guidance and should not be relied upon in that manner. Employers are encouraged to seek legal advice with counsel of their choosing for legal guidance with any workplace law issue. To find out more about these legal principles you can contact the following legal advice websites with organizations:

Alliance Defending Freedom	**Pacific Justice Institute**	**First Liberty**
ADFLegal.org	*pji.org*	*FirstLiberty.org*
Key Contact:	*Key Contact:*	*Key Contact:*
Douglas Napier, Esq.	Brad Dacus, Esq.	Kelly Shackelford, Esq.
Address:	*Address:*	*Address:*
15100 N. 90th StreetScottsdale, AZ 85260	P.O. Box 276600, Sacramento, CA 95827-6600	2001 W. Plano Parkway, Suite 1600, Plano, TX 75075
Phone:	*Phone:*	*Phone:*
(800) 835-5233	(916) 857-6900	(972) 941-4444

Fear #2: What will others think?

In business, there are many stakeholders that are involved, including shareholders, the Board of Directors, the management team, employees, customers, suppliers, etc. The thought that may go through your mind is "what will happen to the business if some or all of these groups of people go against this idea?" Let us deal with some of these groups individually.

Shareholders

As this group controls and owns the business, without their majority consent the idea of operating the business as a ministry based on overtly Christian principles is dead. However if they are concerned about overtly declaring the Christian faith, there is an intermediate step that is not as bold or risky. In other words, the company can be run on the same good values of honesty, integrity, respect, kindness as well as caring and social responsibility, without the public statement of a specific religious belief. Be conscious of the fact that in the end it is all about caring for our neighbor. There is no point in declaring God's love if we do not care for our neighbor. For Jesus taught, "whatever you did for one of the least of these brothers and sisters of mine, you did for me" (Matt. 25:40).

We begin by basing the caring programs on the Golden Rule. This simple concept is shared by many faiths and can establish common ground upon which caring programs can be built. Many such companies have successfully created a mission statement that includes these good values to which they will then attach a statement of their desire to honor God. This is a softer statement as people of faith will agree to the existence of God. Other programs that can easily be implemented are caring committees that focus on such phrases as "caught you caring" and many others that do not have an overtly religious connection. The idea with the softer approach is to start slowly and be committed to the programs and to win the hearts of your employees by showing true and honest care for them.

Once you have demonstrated your true care for them, it follows naturally that you would be concerned for not only their physical well-being, but also their spiritual well-being. Many of these companies, after time, then take an additional step of introducing a corporate chaplain as an employee benefit for those employees who seek emotional/spiritual counseling and support (more on corporate chaplains in Chapter 5).

Management Team

This is the group that runs the day-to-day business. There are many examples of owners who are intent on running the business as a ministry, but do nothing to involve their management team in this process. In many of these cases, this concept then becomes the "owner's thing," with little or no involvement or support from the management team. This can greatly limit the extent to which it is able to impact all levels of the company. For this process to reach its full potential, it is very important that the management team be involved in the creation, implementation and administration. When done properly they will take ownership of it and over time will fully support and own the process. The process will then become "our thing" and become part of the corporate culture. Again, as mentioned above, if there are certain managers that are skeptical, then take the "softer" approach first to begin the process of caring.

Employees

In most companies, the employees' opinions can best be described as a bell curve (pictured below), in which roughly 10% of employees will enthusiastically embrace the concept of Core Values and faith in the work place, while 80% will be initially indifferent and take a "wait and see" attitude, with the remaining 10% being passively resistant. Most human beings want to know that they are valued and cared for, and employees are no different.

CARING COMPANY CULTURE ADOPTION BELL CURVE

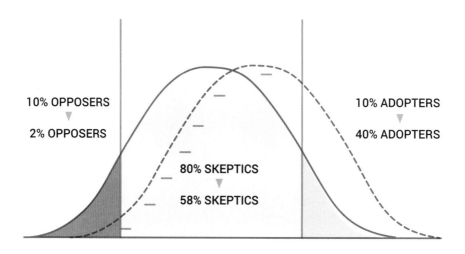

10% OPPOSERS
▼
2% OPPOSERS

10% ADOPTERS
▼
40% ADOPTERS

80% SKEPTICS
▼
58% SKEPTICS

Accordingly, if management is prepared to demonstrate genuine caring for their employees in practical and meaningful ways, people believe what they see happen, not simply what is said. Over time, with good communication and follow through, those that initially were indifferent or even passively resistant begin to warm up to your display of caring and begin to accept and even embrace it and you. If your caring is done in a non-discriminating and respectful manner, the right environment is created for people to be attracted to the source of that love, God Himself.

Fear #3: Will I Lose Customers?

In terms of financial impact to the business, you may think this is the fear that will have the greatest potentially negative impact. However, as was explained in the chapters "Rubber meets the road" and "There is going to be a barbeque, and you are invited" in *The Business Card* book, when the Master of the Universe is recognized as such, your worst fears can be turned into your most pleasant surprises. Over the years, we have heard from HWAW companies that many customers make positive comments about their Core Values. They appreciate knowing that they can rely on the company being faithful to good Core Values and that the values make good business sense. In most cases, customers are less interested or concerned about the statement of religious belief than they are interested in knowing that they can trust the company to deal with them using good values.

Suppliers and competitors often respond in a similar way. Do not underestimate the positive impact that you can have on all of these groups. We form relationships with each of them in the hope that we create win-win benefits for each other. In life, the best relationships are those that are based on the Christian Core Values like honesty, love, respect, and kindness, all of which lead to the building of trust. Trust is the currency of all relationships. The most intimate relationship we have is with our spouse, and most people form this union based on these same Core Values and they consecrate their relationship in a church before God. For some reason though, most people find it difficult to allow God into their interaction with the stakeholders in a business. Is this because we are able to compartmentalize our relationship with our Maker to only be effective on Sundays? Doesn't it seem logical that if we want God in the middle of our most intimate marriage relationship that He would be able to make all our relationships better, including business relationships?

Fear #4: Can I Afford It?

One of the fears most of us have as we start down this path is "If I spend all this money on caring for my employees, will I get anything in return?" Maybe the inverse of this question is more appropriate, "Can I afford NOT to care for my employees?" As one CEO put it, how can you put a cost on the chance to provide Eternal Value? It is truly priceless. Where do we spend our money anyway? Think of the foolishness of the person who spends thousands of dollars in keeping his car in top condition but does not invest in his own health. The best investment we can make is the one in our people, both financially and (most importantly) in terms of EternalROI™.

The main financial spend associated with implementing a Caring Company Culture is the budget for the Caring Team and selected Caring Activities. The budget is determined by the Vision Team, with guidelines on how it is allocated and spent. There is a wide range of cost based on the Caring Activity selected but don't ever forget the most basic Caring Activity is free — a thank you, a smile, a random act of kindness, demonstrating patience, and respect and humility to your 'neighbors'. We will share some details of the Cost Classification of Caring Activities in Chapter 4 or you may contact *hwaw.com* to learn more.

1.3 Define the Vision Team Role and Responsibilities

The role and responsibilities should be defined and shared with each member of the Vision Team.

Role: To help transform the culture of the organization by implementing and living out the HWAW process. Living out the HWAW process through leading by example and by being an example to the rest of the employees. After all, the Vision Team should model desired behaviors.

Responsibilities
- Ensure these 4 critical questions are answered for the organization:
  - ▷ Why do we exist? (Purpose — May be set by the CEO)
  - ▷ What do we do? (Mission)
  - ▷ How will we behave? (Core Values)
  - ▷ What does this look like when living this out?
- Identify the initial Caring Activities to improve or implement (they should point toward your Core Values, i.e. desired behaviors).

- Establish the Caring Team mission, objectives, organization, funding, members and hand-off plan.
- Provide on-going support to the Caring Team.
- Agree on the what 'success' looks like and the key performance indicators (KPIs) that will be reviewed.
- Develop the Communication Plan.
- Develop and own YOUR plan for providing a Caring Company Culture.

In Chapter 5, you will learn how to implement these objectives.

STEP 1 POTENTIAL OBSTACLES

Members of the Vision Team do not support the CEO because they are not of the same faith as the CEO.

Refer to the HWAW Key Concept #4: "How we do this with respect." This concept helps relate the ultimate goal of transforming the company culture across a multi-cultural workforce that represents many denominations of the Christian faith, other religions, and even no faith.

We worked with a company in the manufacturing industry that was putting together the Vision Team. The team had a non-Christian top executive and the CEO was tempted to not invite that executive into the Vision Team for fear of generating a potentially hostile atmosphere. After consulting with HWAW Coaches, we recommended quite the opposite. We believe you should include this executive on the Vision Team because it will be easier to care for and love and, thus, understand that person if he is nearer, rather than if he is outside the Vision Team. The company followed the advice and this executive has become a strong supporter of the HWAW movement within the company.

Delay in addressing concerns from leadership will only lead to bigger issues later in the process. Being able to address concerns from the Vision Team is a good test to know if you are ready to address concerns from all levels of the organization. Think of your Vision Team as your very critical pilot team.

We realize we need help.

If you encounter roadblocks that you do not feel prepared to handle, resources are available to support you at *hwaw.com*.

Signs that would indicate we should not move forward yet.

Potential signs include:

- If the CEO says he is all-in and ready to go, but he is not giving the time or support to the transformation plan. Then, you should have a candid discussion with the CEO before moving forward.

- If someone on the Vision Team is very disruptive or negative at this point, then you may need to make sure you understand the drivers of frustration or fear and schedule time for a candid discussion with this team member and the CEO.

- If the CEO or Vision Team supports the process, but have some general concerns about their personal barriers to implementation, then you should thank them for letting you know and provide some time to help them through this.

Dealing with Personal Barriers to Implementation

While in the process of evaluating whether or not to pursue the concept of running a business as a platform for ministry and basing it on Christian principles and values, there are many barriers that come to mind that must be thought of and overcome. The main barriers for Peter Friessle were as follows:

Am I worthy?
"Was I worthy to be the moral/spiritual leader of our business?" As I had spent 3 days at the retreat evaluating my life, I realized just how much junk I had been hiding in the rooms of my soul and how badly I had treated those neighbors in my life. I was so embarrassed. Having realized my weaknesses and failings, and that pride was my number one weakness, how could I now go in front of all these people and assume the role of a moral leader? I began to pray and ask God for the wisdom and courage to assume this new role. The answer came in the simple understanding of my responses to two questions:

- Did I truly believe that God had forgiven me?
- Did I trust with all my heart that He could and would support me in this mission He laid before me?

Forgiveness
I knew with my whole heart that God had forgiven me; it felt like a 10-ton

weight had been lifted off my shoulders. This was the most incredible and liberating feeling I had ever felt. To use the words of John MacArthur, "Forgiveness unleashes joy. It brings peace. It washes the slate clean. It sets all the highest values of love in motion." But what about those people I had hurt in the past? Would they forgive me? If not, would I be held captive? I thought back to the old adage about unforgiving hearts, "Harboring grievances is like taking poison yourself and then waiting for your enemy to die!" If those that I had hurt were unwilling to forgive, there was nothing I could do, other than pray for a softening of their heart. I realized that the past was the past and that living in the past was the surest way to lock God and everyone else out of my present. So I proceeded to assume this new mission, but I knew I had to ask those I had knowingly and unknowingly hurt for forgiveness, and in humility, ask for their patience as I committed myself to strive to follow God's way more closely. (I say strive, because I knew that in my humanness, that there were going to be times when I would fail, and so I was not committing to be perfect but rather to making an authentic effort).

Trust

Trust is a simple concept until you are put to the test. As a businessman, I, for years, had felt like the success of the business was directly related to my efforts. To now go on this new journey where I was handing over the reins to someone I could not even see or touch, who I would be proclaiming as the new Boss, and running the business according to His principles, I thought, "Wow I really had to trust Him!" The fact that this had the very real potential of negatively impacting my customers, employees, vendors and the overall success of the business was really scary. The time had come. I was on the edge of the cliff and I had to decide if I was going to jump or not. As so beautifully stated in Psalm139…"Trust in the Lord with all your heart and lean not on your own understanding, in all ways acknowledge Him and He will make your path straight." I leapt…

STEP 1 SUCCESSES

The Vision Team understands where the CEO wants to go and is able to share the story when asked.

One CEO described his journey as wanting to *leave significance* when he retired. He described what significance meant to him in a way that members of the Vision Team could understand and share his unique story with others.

Fears are openly shared and discussed.

One member of an all-Christian Vision Team was worried how supervisors would take this if they were not Christian. He shared a story of an excellent supervisor that was from another country and believed in his local gods and religions. This made the Vision Team think about how to minimize fears around promotion and growth opportunities for non-Christians.

Team members first think of what they need to do differently to fulfill roles and responsibilities.

Team members shared what they needed to do differently personally and as leaders in the company to uphold these responsibilities before trying to change the rest of the company. They even worked with HR to identify development tools and education to help them grow where they had their own opportunities.

STEP 1 PROCESS CHECK

- [ ] The Vision Team has been defined.

- [ ] The CEO has shared where he is and where he wants to go on the His Way at Work journey.

- [ ] HWAW key concepts have been reviewed with the Vision Team.

- [ ] The assessments have been completed and reviewed with the Vision Team.

- [ ] Potential fears have been addressed and reduced or eliminated.

- [ ] The role and responsibilities of the Vision Team have been defined and reviewed.

NOTES

STEP TWO

Create Your Transformation Plan

LEADER'S PRAYER

Dear Lord,

Thank You for being with me during this journey so far. Thank You for strength to be transparent to others about my love for You and the courage to persevere even when I wonder if I am really ready or even worthy. Thank You for the strength to see everyone through Your eyes as they support, question, or oppose me on this journey. I ask that You please touch the hearts of those that may be questioning or opposing this journey so that one day they will get to know You as I do and understand my ultimate purpose for wanting to create Eternal Value.

As I begin the planning phase with my Vision Team, please stay by our sides to make sure we are making the right decisions for You and are doing Your will as You would like for it to be done. Please help us remember that even though we know having a good plan is an important part of creating a Caring Company Culture with excellence, we realize we must be flexible and faithful knowing our plans will continue to be impacted by spiritual warfare. I am committing myself to You now that I will not give up!

> *"The Sovereign Lord is my strength."*
> HABAKKUK 3:19

Please help me to remember that I am not in this alone and I can turn to You at any time for discernment and prayer and that HWAW is here for me also. In the end, all of the success from this journey is for YOU.

In Your Name,
Amen

1 *Align the Vision Team* — CEO

2 *Create Your Implementation Plan* — VISION TEAM

3 *Cascade Engagement* — CARING TEAM

4 *Live Out His Way at Work* — COMMUNITIES, FAMILIES, & EMPLOYEES

We were working with a company that provides design, construction, civil engineering, and related professional services. The CEO was a spiritual man who was 'quiet' about his faith and not sure how to share it inside a company. Fortunately, his wife was not so quiet and she wanted him to be comfortable sharing more inside his company. After she heard Peter speak and learned about HWAW, she convinced her husband to let HWAW help him understand how he can love his employees, their families, and the community like Jesus while letting them know that he does this to Honor God. Over the next 12 months, we were blessed to help them through Steps 2.1–2.6 and be able to watch beautiful outcomes unfold.

What is Step 2?

This section is about the process of developing your own plan for transforming your company culture. We will use the results of the assessments and the lessons in Step 1 to create your own implementation plan.

2.1 Develop Purpose, Mission and Core Values

2.2 Conduct Caring Matrix Assessment

2.3 Define Initial Caring Team

2.4 Define KPIs

Develop Communication Plan

Summarize Implementaiton Plan

Why complete Step 2?

It may sound very formal and traditional, but the experience we have accumulated since 2006 tells us that in order to truly transform your culture, a consistent methodology is required. This will allow the CEO to manage the organization's culture as a priority with a plan and process in place. We developed the process as if you are starting from scratch, but where you are in your journey will determine which steps are required for your company and where you can start. We have proven that not only will this process work to help you promote a caring company culture where you can create Eternal Value, this process will also help you expedite the execution of the transformation and save you painful lessons that would otherwise be part of the normal learning curve.

We recognize this journey is part of a bigger plan and it will require much discernment, faith and courage, which will ultimately determine the speed of implementation. Most importantly though, this is not a destination, it is a journey; so, you and only you will be able to judge the right speed at which you want and will implement it.

Most journeys have only one target with a finite ending. The beauty of this journey is that if we sincerely love our neighbors, the journey will never end... it is eternal!

HOW TO COMPLETE STEP 2

2.1 Develop the Purpose, Mission and Core Values

There are four simple and very important questions requiring discernment before moving forward. If you already have answered them, we recommend that you take some time to confirm they are still valid within the scope of this journey.

- Why does your organization exist?
- What does your organization do?
- How does your organization behave?
- What does your organization look like when living this vision?

To answer these questions, we turned to the brilliant business leaders Jim Collins, Patrick Lencioni, Jim Kouzes, Barry Posner, and Ken Blanchard and their teachings on how each of these are defined and developed. For the purpose of this guide, we are going to integrate our lessons from them and use the following terms to describe the answer to each of these questions.

- **Purpose:** Why does your organization exist?
- **Mission:** What does your organization do?
- **Core Values and Behaviors**: How does your organization behave?
- **Metrics and Goals:** What does your organization look like when living this vision?

HWAW offers a unique Purpose, Mission and Core Value workshop to help your Vision Team work through these 4 questions. If you would like to learn more, visit *hwaw.com*.

IMPLEMENTATION PLAN

Purpose	Mission	Core Values
Why you exist	*What you do*	*How you behave*
Goals	Metrics	Behaviors
What gets measured, gets done.	*Measure behaviors, not values.*	*Habits: Virtues or Vices?*

What is a Company's Purpose?

This is the deepest, most important question to be answered. However, it is also the most recent question of the four to be answered in a formal way by businesses. When we started HWAW, asking "why do we exist?" was not as common for company leaders as it is today. Yet, we have found it helps CEOs focus on why they are here doing what they do and explain it to the Vision Team and employees. Your Purpose is your ultimate reason for being a company and company owner. Once you understand your purpose, it should transcend over time. Something to think about: A human being's purpose is to serve God. A company is comprised of people. Shouldn't a company's purpose also be to serve God…in some way?

Answer each of the following for Purpose:
1. Why do we exist?
2. What are the key words and their meanings for our organization?

Donnelly Communications' Purpose
To honor God and live our values, thereby earning the trust
of leading companies, gaining the privilege to serve their
customers, and enriching the lives of our employees.

*Donnelly Communications (donnellycommunications.com) is a pioneer in the
outsourced contact center industry with headquarters in Atlanta, Georgia.*

Visit hwaw.com/guideresources *to see more examples of Company Purpose.*

What is a Mission?

A Mission is a one-sentence statement or phrase describing what the
organization does day-to-day that is used to help guide decisions about
priorities, actions, and responsibilities.

Answer each of the following to determine your company's Mission:
- What do we do?
- What are the key words and their meanings for our organization?

Our Company Mission
Qualfon's mission is to help as many people as
possible pursue their total vocation — as individuals and
as members of society — by creating an ever-growing number
of job opportunities as we strive to become the outsourcer
of choice for our clients. In summary, our mission is
"Be the Best BPO. Make People's Lives Better."

*Qualfon (qualfon.com), is a global provider of contact center, back-office, and
business process outsourcing (BPO) services with locations across the globe.*

Visit hwaw.com/guideresources *to see more examples of Company Mission.*

What are Your Core Values?

Core Values are the few (3–4) key values by which we live our life. They describe how we behave. Our true Core Values are the principles we use to guide us in our decisions, and help us in those crossroads of life where we might be pulled in opposing directions.

Core Values should be specific and well defined so that we can make clear, informed decisions when we encounter these crossroads. Ideally, those around us can identify our Core Values by our very habits and behaviors.

Beliefs vs. Values vs. Behaviors

We find it is helpful for your team and employees to understand the difference between beliefs, values and behaviors before defining them.

Beliefs: an opinion or conviction; confidence in the truth or existence of something not immediately susceptible to rigorous proof, confidence; faith; trust or a religious creed or faith.

Values: important and lasting beliefs or ideals shared by the members of a culture about what is good or bad and desirable or undesirable. Virtues: morally good behavior or character, moral excellence.

Behaviors: observable activity in a human, the manner of conducting oneself. Behaviors are measurable.

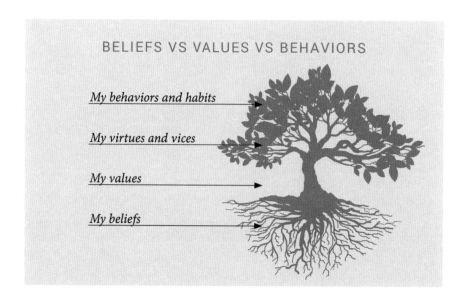

Why have Core Values?

As a CEO from one of our HWAW companies said during the Core Value workshop, "Many of you have heard me say: 'when you have a difficult decision to make, use your values,' when in doubt, your values will guide you. And that happens to all of us but if you follow your values, your decision will be the right one."

One CEO shared this story with his Vision Team: "The company our parents founded operated with excellence and adhered to its Core Values. That is what kept the company alive and growing for 40 years, even when the industry's natural cycles sent us all through difficult times, we were able to endure because our Core Values inspired our employees to work, even without pay for months at a time. They believed in the company's leadership and, thus, eventually, when the cycles came back up, the company (and its employees) reaped the benefits of holding on."

Another HWAW CEO reminded his team during a Core Value workshop that "Companies may have executives that are even willing to quit because the company's values are not in line with those of the person. We are not doing this to just celebrate at the end of the year with a party, we want to do it every day with conviction."

Answer each of the following for Core Values:
1. How do we behave?
2. What are the key words and their meanings for our organization?
3. What do model behaviors look like for any employee in the organization?

Example of Core Values and Behaviors from a HWAW Company:

Hampton Farms Values
The acronym "EQUIP" guides everything that we do each day.

Environment
Protecting God's Creation and Promoting Excellence in our Work Environment

Quality
Reflecting the Highest Quality and Care in All Products and Services

Understanding
Understanding Employee Needs for a Balanced Work-Personal Life; Promoting a Family-Friendly Workplace

Integrity
Honoring God by Conducting All Business with Honesty and Integrity

People
Promoting a Workplace, Encouraging Creative Solutions from Our Most Important Asset, Our People

Hampton Farms (hamptonfarms.com) is a large producer of peanuts and other products in the US.

For more examples of Company Core Values and Behaviors, go to hwaw.com/guideresources.

How do you know if you are living these behaviors?

As one HWAW CEO shared, "If you only have your Core Values on a sign on the wall and you stop there, then why have them? The reason for having them is to help guide decisions, actions and behaviors of all employees in the company every day. If we truly want to live by them, then we need to know how well we are living them. How do YOU know if you are living them?"

Another CEO shared this with his team as they discussed faith in the HWAW Core Value, Purpose and Mission workshop:

> *"How do we make this program something that we combine with our day to day? Today's work is fully spiritual, so it may feel awkward to be so operational and make us stop and think spiritually. We want to be guided on how to integrate spirituality into the day-to-day so that we keep our regular ROI KPIs, but yet we keep in mind something that is actually MORE important, which is the spirituality (our EternalROI™ KPIs). This is a big change for the company; we are now having the opportunity to find our spiritual North and not just our operational North. This is regardless of the religion we may have, this is voluntary and from our hearts. This is not something we are pushing down the throat of our co-workers. This is about a bigger Being, a Force that is beyond us."*

CORE VALUES AT WORK

2.2 Conduct the Caring Matrix Assessment

THE CARING MATRIX:

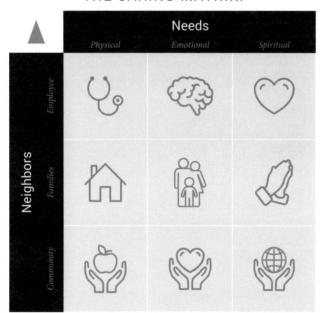

What is a HWAW Caring Matrix?

It is the unique tool for identifying ways to care for employees, their families, and communities by helping to meet physical, emotional, and spiritual needs. It is the primary vehicle for deciding how to best cascade engagement of caring across the organization (both inside and out).

The Caring Matrix helps the organization identify and communicate how best to care for each other and be consistent with the Purpose, Mission and Core Values. Some companies choose to start the process with Step 2.2 and then go back to Step 2.1 because they feel it is a more tangible way to show caring than the words alone in the Core Values, Mission and Purpose statement. HWAW recommends companies NOT do that if at all possible.

Companies should first have clearly defined values, purpose and mission so that the Caring Matrix can be used to support them and, in doing so, transform the organization's culture.

What is a Caring Activity?

A Caring Activity is sponsored by the organization and demonstrates living out Core Values through physical, emotional and/or spiritual caring for employees, families and/or communities. HWAW classifies Caring Activities into 3 categories: Reach, Need and Stage.

Classifications:

1. **By Reach** *(The people we are caring for)*
   - Employees
   - Families
   - Communities

2. **By Need** *(The needs we are trying to meet)*
   - Physical
   - Emotional
   - Spiritual

3. **By Stage** *(The way we are trying to care in the employee's growth process)*
   - Relief *(reactive)*
   - Rehabilitative
   - Development *(proactive)*

Caring Activities should offer options that appeal to all employees. We recognize that each person is different and may have different needs at various times in their lives. In order to provide a Caring Activity that will reach each employee, it is important that you truly know each employee, their families and the community in which they live and work in order to know their physical, emotional and spiritual needs. The Caring Matrix provides the process to do this, but it must be supported by an environment that encourages leaders to know their employees and for employees to get to know each other.

What are the key Caring Activities we recommend to start with at the Company level?

- Corporate Chaplain
- Chapel or place where employees can go to pray or spend time with the chaplain
- Some form of an Employee Assistance Fund

Chaplain Program

A vital aspect of a Caring Corporate Culture is assuring that each and every employee is ministered to on an individual basis. Research tells us that up to 70% of people in the workplace do not have a pastor. While "pastor" is often considered a religious term, the ancient use of the word translated "pastor" is "one who cares for the flock." Our "flock," our employees, need a confidential source of care and spiritual guidance. Over the past two decades, corporate chaplains have been utilized in organizations, large and small, both private and public companies, and in organizations that are driving a spiritual agenda, as well as companies merely seeking to provide care for their employees.

The most popular model for corporate chaplaincy involves a designated chaplain that calls on the company weekly. Over time, this chaplain will build relationships with employees, establishing trust. This trust allows the employees to confide in their corporate chaplain during times of need. While some organizations directly employ a corporate chaplain, His Way at Work encourages you to consider an outside source for chaplaincy. Our experience is that this outside source provides a critical level of confidentiality that significantly raises the level of employee trust.

Corporate chaplains assist employees in times of stress, loss of a loved one, illness, and dealing with issues of substance abuse. Employee participation is voluntary. The corporate chaplain serves as a valued representative of the organization for hospital visitation, as well as at funerals and even prison.

Corporate Chaplaincy Today:

- There are at least 5,000 full and part-time chaplains.
- Chaplaincy agencies in the U.S. have been growing at double-digit annual rates for at least a decade.
- Corporate chaplain programs currently operate in all fifty U.S. states as well as in Canada, Mexico, Asia, Africa, Europe, Australia, and the Pacific Rim.
- Chaplaincies support companies with as few as 25 employees and as many as 125,000.
- Practically every industry in the U.S. is being served.
- No legal hurdles stand in the way of having a chaplain program when conducted under the Chaplain Program Guidelines used by chaplaincy organizations.

His Way at Work enjoys a strategic partnership with Corporate Chaplains of America, one of the leading corporate chaplaincy organizations in the nation. There are other organizations that provide the same service in the US like Marketplace Chaplains. For assistance in finding a chaplain outside of the U.S., please contact us at *hwaw.com*. We can provide valuable guidance in the consideration of your corporate chaplain.

Chapel

The Chapel is a place to allow people to connect to God through prayers, worship, Bible studies, quiet time and time with your chaplain. A chapel is important to foster people's connection to God through prayers and worship and has the following three objectives:

- Creating a culture of prayer in the company.
- Integrating faith in the workplace by providing a safe space for employees to pray and seek God.
- Allowing employees to have a devotional or solitary time with God to strengthen their spiritual lives.

Chapel activities must be voluntary, accommodating, and non-discriminatory. Some resources that are useful in the chapel include Bibles, spiritual books, devotional books and a prayer request box. If you cannot afford or do not have the space for a chapel, do not worry! Many HWAW companies convert an area in an existing building into a chapel or prayer room. At the minimum, you can purchase prayer benches and place them in certain locations or make them easily accessible.

Employee Assistance Fund

The Employee Emergency Assistance Fund is designed to provide limited financial assistance to employees who are experiencing economic hardship due to certain emergency situations. Although it differs between companies and cultures, this fund usually serves two objectives. One is to provide financial support through loans to employees facing an emergency or difficult times. The other is to serve employees and demonstrate care and support to overcome difficulties, bringing peace of mind to the employees and their families.

Some examples of emergency situations are:
- A personal or family crisis involving an emergency financial need or an unexpected medical expense which exceed insurance provisions, resulting in economic hardship.
- Uninsured loss due to fire, which resulted in economic hardship.
- Funeral cost for the death of an uninsured dependent family member.

Companies may also choose to offer financial counseling to the employee who submits an application for assistance.

What is the next level of Caring Activity?

The next level should be determined by the Caring Team. Once you go through Step 2 at the Vision Team level, you will continue to go through these steps at the Caring Team level. This is one way the Vision Team passes the ownership of caring to the Caring Team and employees.

Examples of Caring Activities:
- Running activity
- Corporate chaplain
- I Caught You Caring
- Chapel
- Library for adults and children
- Voluntary prayer/devotion time at work
- Coin recognition/reminder/team building program
- Local ministries invited to Caring Team meeting
- Marriage enrichment retreats
- Family planning education
- Local/overseas short and long term mission trips

- Continuing education
- Personal financial management training
- Bible study
- Medical screenings
- Addiction cessation programs
- Substance abuse rehab
- Volunteer hours program
- Celebrate with Gratitude! (birthday and anniversary meeting)
- Compassionate Severance Plan
- Aging family support groups
- Sponsor employee family activities
- Display a HWAW plaque at the reception desk area
- Join a small team of fellow CEO's
- Establishment of initial fund for Caring Activities based profit sharing
- Emergency employee fund
- Benevolent fund
- Car repair fund
- Loan fund
- Employee home repair fund
- General and community charity fund
- Communicate mission/values through a coin
- Communicate mission/values through business cards
- Communicate mission/values through a poster
- Monthly newsletter
- Weekly inspirational phrase
- Texting strategies
- Parenting courses
- Adoption
- Single parenting conferences
- Educational recognition and scholarship for employee's children
- Baby sitter and movie ticket for new moms
- Prayer groups for employees, clients, suppliers, and others
- Covenant Eyes
- Establish mission statement with religious principles
- Define Core Values with religious principles
- Invite other CEO's and Executives to experience the company
- Send employee's children to Christian or religious-based camps
- Use religious leaders as motivational speakers at company meetings
- Hold annual provider and client appreciation outings

- Hire disadvantaged people including former criminals, etc.
- Provide discounted/free services to pastors and other religious leaders
- Drives for baby items for new moms

To access these Caring Activities and guidelines, go to *hwaw.com*. For more ideas, refer to 102 Ministry Ideas from C12 Group located in the Appendix. These are included with permission from C12 Group.

How do you know the needs today of your employees, their families and the community? What can you do differently to ensure you know the needs in the future?

> *"To love your people you need to care for your people and to care for your people you must know your people first, because you cannot love what you don't know."*
> — MOTHER TERESA

Identify the Caring Activities you already offer.

Most companies already offer some form of Caring Activities, whether they are aware of it or not. The objective of our Caring Matrix assessment is to help the Vision Team get aligned on what they already offer. Start by identifying the Caring Activities that you offer as a company (formally or informally) and plot them in the block in the Caring Matrix where they fit best. If you have a Caring Activity that fits in more than one block, write it so that it crosses all the blocks that are applicable.

YOUR CURRENT CARING MATRIX:

	Needs		
	Physical	Emotional	Spiritual
Employee			
Families			
Community			

Neighbors

Next, collect the cost, number of souls impacted, and the process used to manage the activity (we will call these Caring Activity guidelines in future steps) to help you determine the effectiveness of each activity and the current role in the budget (is it in the budget, is it under budget or is it over budget). The objective is to ensure the Vision Team has a comprehensive picture of the existing Caring Activities, budget, reach and process.

EXAMPLE: CARING TEAM METRICS

2015 Caring Funds	Jan	Feb	March	April	May	June
General Fund	($54)	$1,495	$736	$976	$1,086	$2,643
Benevolent (company match)	$7,180	$3,506	$2,804	$3,466	$5,560	$3,258
Home Repairs	$0	$1,073	$2,166	$4,331	$4,927	$6,497
Car Towing Service	$0	$206	$585	$100	$251	$269
Car Repairs	$1,993	$3,093	$0	$730	$2,165	$2,701
Medical Funds	$650	$216	$866	$433	$434	$216
"Reach Out"	$0	$500	$750	$1,240	$370	$500
Community Charity	$3,000	$3,000	$3,000	$3,000	$3,000	$3,000
Employee Gift Cards	$0	$0	$0	$0	$10,925	$0
Total	$12,769	$13,089	$10,907	$14,276	$28,718	$19,084
Budget	$16,750	$16,750	$16,750	$28,750	$16,750	$16,750

Employees	Jan	Feb	Mar	Apr	May	Jun	Jul	Aug	Total	Goal
Caught You Caring										
# of "Caught you Carings"	10	10	15	15	15	23	0	0	88	185
# of Empl. Caught Caring	15	12	17	24	24	24	0	0	116	265
"Caring Concerns"										
Reports	3	4	3	3	4	6	3	0	26	40
Bible/Life Studies										
# of Keeping Pace mtgs.	4	4	5	4	4	5	4	2	32	48
# Attending	166	164	222	217	181	220	168	82	1,420	1,920
Average Attending	42	41	44	54	45	44	42	41	44	40
YouTube Channel views	11	22	13	25	16	20	22	0	129	350
Employee Development										
English Classes (USA)	0	0	0	3	4	4	4	0	15	0
English Classes (Chile)	4	4	3	0	0	0	0	0	11	4

Lesson Learned: Don't assume your entire Vision Team already knows this information. When we started, we assumed the leadership was aware of what was in place, how much was being spent, and how many people were impacted. We were amazed at how often members of the leadership (and employees) did not know the full picture. This information is helpful to make sure the leadership is aligned, but also to build on and communicate as part of the journey.

Identify any Caring Activity that you want to eliminate or improve.

Now that you have completed your Caring Matrix, you will want to take steps to improve it by eliminating redundant or inefficient activities and by adding activities to fill unmet needs (the blank spaces in your Caring Matrix). The objective of this exercise is to spend some time thinking about the data you just collected to determine if you want to make any changes before moving forward. What is the data telling you? Are you spending most of the money on an activity that has no reach? Are there activities that no one is participating in, but it takes a lot of time and cost to manage the process? If so, make decisions on activities to eliminate or improve them.

Identify 1–3 Caring Activities you want to add and implement.

Every time we lead a team through the Caring Matrix assessment, it is very obvious to the team where they need to focus, given the gaps that show up in the Caring Matrix. The team will come to this conclusion without anyone having to tell them. The "Pareto Principle," also known as the "80/20 rule," kicks in naturally.

1. Focus on blocks with no activities and begin to identify potential activities that would work for your organization and culture. If all the blocks are blank, we recommend starting by identifying activities that help ensure basic physical needs are fulfilled before moving directly to the spiritual.
2. Focus on blocks with only one or two activities.
3. Leave the rest alone for now. Once the responsibility for Caring Activities is handed off to the Caring Team in Step 3, they will begin to continually assess and review the effectiveness of the Caring Activities and recommend changes.

Often a team will identify many great ideas and want to begin implementing them immediately. You will need to help them prioritize and think about how they fit into the overall plan and the budget that will be established in the next step.

When you are working with a team that is now aware of the gaps and very excited to start adding new activities, it is very tempting to just get started. One of the companies we worked with had gaps across the Spiritual column of the Caring Matrix. They wanted to have the company leader begin to send a weekly Bible verse to all the employees in the company. They started doing this before the employees knew anything about HWAW, the Caring Matrix, Caring Activities, etc. Although most of the employees appreciated the weekly verses, some were asking "what is going on?" Make sure to develop your Communication Plan before you jump in or else it could have an impact on the company's transformation. We will help you develop your Communication Plan in Step 2.5.

How do you want to implement these 1–3 initiatives?

For each Caring Activity identified to eliminate, improve or add, capture the specific tasks required, the owner, the due date and the cost (if applicable). This will become part of the larger Implementation Plan in future steps. This is also important to help the Vision Team understand the timing in preparation of the Communication Plan.

Note: Do not assume that if a Caring Activity works for one company, it will work in every company. It must fit the needs of the neighbors in your company. When we started sharing the HWAW process, company leaders would begin implementing the Caring Activities that were successful at Polydeck into their company. Some of them did not work because they did not fit their needs and they had to eliminate them. Do your best to find the right Caring Activities that fit and then use your Caring Team to help monitor if they are working or not for the long term.

Making The Caring Matrix Your Own
We share a basic Caring Matrix, but the x and y axis can look different based on the company's mission and needs. Some companies have a 4x4 or 4x5 Caring Matrix because they added neighbors and needs that make sense for them. For example, some companies prefer to add a need column for Intellectual and some prefer to add a neighbors row for Customers. It will resonate better with your neighbor base if you make it your own.

2.3 Develop Your Caring Team

Your Caring Team will be the eyes, ears and hands of your Core Values. They have responsibility for the development, execution, and oversight of any number of Caring Activities. This is the heart of the HWAW transformation journey. There are seven steps to develop your Caring Team.

1. Develop your Caring Team mission.
2. Define the organization structure, roles and guidelines for the team.
3. Select the initial Caring Team members.
4. Determine the budget.
5. Determine the agenda.
6. Determine metrics for the Caring Activities.
7. Develop the plan for the hand off — how to communicate with the new team.

Develop your Caring Team mission.

Just like the mission for your company, the mission for your Caring Team should reflect what you want the Caring Team to do. Although the mission should be similar for all Caring Teams, how you choose to develop and capture it in writing may be unique to your company.

Example of a Caring Team Mission
Our Caring Team promotes an environment where:

- Core Values and social responsibilities are lived out and experienced in daily operations.
- People are encouraged and given opportunities to improve their workplace, physical health, mental and spiritual growth.
- People trust and support each other in a caring family manner.
- People are encouraged to explore and apply their potential to realize their dreams.
- People are involved beyond their daily work duties and actively participate in shaping the corporate culture and supporting our communities.
- All this is done in a legal, non-discriminatory and non-threatening way.

Define the organizational structure and roles for your Caring Team.

The Caring Team's organizational structure should be designed to best fit your company size, locations and work style. The design should encourage ownership and engagement by the Caring Team. Defining your Caring Team's organizational structure requires dedicated time and attention — this cannot be taken lightly or thrown together on a whim. It does not mean that once this is determined it can never change. It should continue to evolve and improve as the team learns and grows, but make sure to take time to think through the initial design and roles.

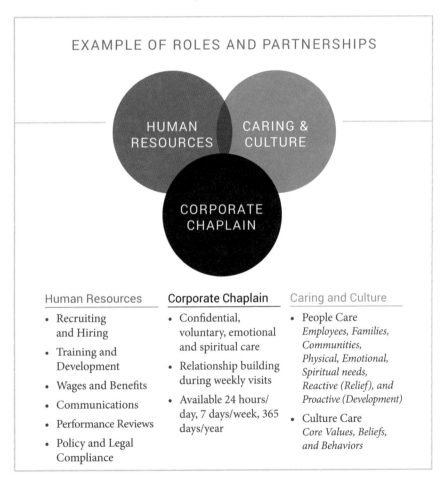

EXAMPLE OF ROLES AND PARTNERSHIPS

HUMAN RESOURCES

CARING & CULTURE

CORPORATE CHAPLAIN

Human Resources	Corporate Chaplain	Caring and Culture
• Recruiting and Hiring	• Confidential, voluntary, emotional and spiritual care	• People Care *Employees, Families, Communities, Physical, Emotional, Spiritual needs, Reactive (Relief), and Proactive (Development)*
• Training and Development	• Relationship building during weekly visits	
• Wages and Benefits	• Available 24 hours/ day, 7 days/week, 365 days/year	• Culture Care *Core Values, Beliefs, and Behaviors*
• Communications		
• Performance Reviews		
• Policy and Legal Compliance		

The first role to define is the Caring Team leader. What is required in this role? What are the specific duties? How long does it take to complete the duties each month? Will this person vote?

How is this role different than the role of an HR leader? How does it link with the HR leader? How is this role different than the role of the Corporate Chaplain? How does it link with the Corporate Chaplain?

Is the Caring Team leader going to be a role a current employee handles on the side, a full time role, or a role facilitated by a HWAW coach? Who is the right person to fill this role?

If possible, we recommend that each department or group within your company should have a representative on the Caring Team. If a department or group is too small, that department can be included with peer departments. It is essential that employees feel like they are being represented by the Caring Team members. This will be critical in the success of cascading engagement across the organization as you begin to execute.

EXAMPLES OF CARING TEAM ORGANIZATIONS

Company A

Company B

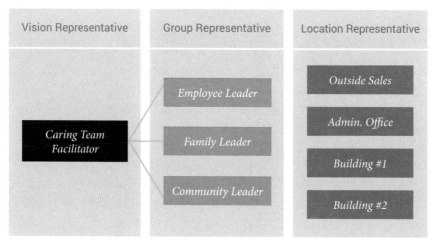

Company C

Chief Mission Office Verticals
Communication at Work: **Promotes an environment where people are encouraged and have the opportunity to share in the company's mission and understand the organization's values, plans and goals.**
Learn at Work: **Promotes an environment where people are developed to explore and apply their full vocation.**
Care at Work: **Promotes an environment where people trust and support each other in caring family manner.**
Give at Work: **Promotes an environment where people are involved beyond what their daily work duties require of them and actively participate in supporting the needs of our communities.**
Fun at Work: **Transforms Qualfon into an environment full of opportunities to share common hobbies and interests, learn and have fun.**

To learn more about the Mission Office structure and Mission Officer Job Description, visit *hwaw.com/guideresources*.

Select the Initial Team Members.

Your organizational structure will determine the number of team members, the group they represent and the role they will play. We recommend taking nominations from the areas and then allowing them to make the final selection of the team member from their area. Having members who are respected by their peers is a formula for success, especially in your initial Caring Team.

Determine the Budget.

The Vision Team determines the budget for the Caring Team and Caring Activities. Vision Teams may decide to use a percentage of sales or profit or what they can afford given their financial situation. Once the budget is established, the team will need to determine how this budget will be allocated across the Caring Matrix and how it will be managed and tracked during the year. Depending on the size of the Caring Team, there may be a person identified as the 'accountant' to perform this role or this may be assigned to the Caring Team facilitator.

Generally, we recommend the budget start with 80% employees, 19% families, and 1% communities and eventually move to: 60% employees, 30% families, and 10% communities or what feels right for that company and location.

Consider:

- How much will be available in the budget to support Caring Activities?
- How will this be allocated across groups?
- Who is responsible for managing and tracking budget to actual spend?
- What would be the best way to move the funds to support not only the entire Caring Program but specifically the Caring Team? Some companies set up a Foundation (501c3) to transfer the funds to and then the Foundation moves the money to pay for some (or all) of the Caring Program needs. Some other companies transfer the funds to a Community Foundation and specify where the funds need to be transferred. We recommend you to talk with your accountant to make it part of your company's fiscal strategy.

Develop Guidelines for your Caring Team

- Pay rates/scales are not to be discussed.
- Benefits are not to be discussed.
- There should be no criticism of a particular individual.
- Team structure is set by the Vision Team.
- Term on the team is set by the Vision Team.
- Clear expectations are set for the Caring Team.
- Treat cases anonymously to avoid favoritism and protect privacy.

Caring Team Meeting Agenda Example

Each Caring Team should develop a meeting schedule, agenda and follow up plan that meets the need of that company and team. Here is one example.

- Open in prayer.
- Present the money raised in the previous activity.
- Present a non-profit organization.
- Vote if the Caring Team will provide any assistance to the non-profit (financial or volunteer).
- Update of budget and current spending.
- Follow up on each Caring Program.
- Present and discuss each Key Performance Indicator.
- Plan the next events.

- Vote on each individual case of loans or donations from the Caring Funds.
- Make time for new ideas.
- Set schedule for the next meeting.

Caring Team Metrics

The Caring Team should use the resources set in the Caring Team budget to create Eternal Value by striving to honor God through programs focused on employees, families, and community. The Caring Team should create metrics and Key Performance Indicators (KPIs) to measure the impact of each one of the activities. These KPIs also should be connected to the company's overall goals. Each KPI should have a goal to be achieved in a certain period of time (forecast for 5 years).

Some examples of KPIs are:
- Loans (financial amount and quantity)
- Donations (financial amount and quantity)
- Employee volunteer hours
- Chaplain contacts

Develop the Plan for the Vision Team Hand-off

As discussed in Section 2, the Vision Team is responsible for handing off the ownership of the Caring Activities to the Caring Team. There are several items that need to be considered in developing the plan for the hand-off, including how you will create a meeting environment that promotes open feedback and engagement and what guidelines will be provided.

Although the Caring Team will own most of the Caring Activities after the hand-off, there are some specific ones that should remain with the Vision Team. You will want to clarify these during the hand-off meeting. Examples may include decisions involving capital or resources like adding a chaplain or equipment and building a chapel.

Things to Consider for an Effective Hand-off:
- Set the environment.
- Ensure all members of the Vision Team are available for the hand-off meeting.
- Ensure all members of the Caring Team are available for the hand-off meeting.

- Schedule the meeting in a comfortable place for both teams.
- Plan a warm welcome as the Caring Team members arrive.
- Organize seating to integrate Vision Team and Caring Team members.
- Open in prayer.
- Ask the CEO to share a "why we are here" introduction that includes his journey, the Purpose and Core Values.
- Include time to review the mission, guidelines, organizational structure, team roles, and responsibilities.
- Hold a mock Caring Team meeting with real examples from other companies.
- Include a calendar with next steps.
- Let them know how special they are.
- Arrange for someone to take pictures use in communications.
- Solicit feedback.
- Listen and answer with honesty and humility.

To purchase a Caring Team manual, visit *hwaw.com*.

2.4 Define Key Performance Indicators for your Purpose, Mission and Core Values.

Key Performance Indicators (KPIs) are the metrics you keep in front of you to see if the transformation journey is making progress. They should include both ROI and EternalROI™ metrics. What KPIs do you currently review to know if you are living out your Purpose, Mission and Core Values? What KPIs can you review to know if you are living out your Purpose, Mission and Core Values for the future?

Here are some common EternalROI™ KPIs used by HWAW Companies:
- Assess Purpose and Core Value behaviors through existing annual company surveys or in a customized way for your company (through a weekly or bi-monthly survey)
- Use your Caring Team metrics:
  — Volunteer hours
  — Participation rate
  — # of Salvations
  — Turnover
  — Purpose or Mission specific measures

Qualfon has 4 Mission metrics that they use as KPIs to assess whether they are reaching their mission.

QUALFON MISSION INDEX

February 2015 Results			
Job Creation	Keep you at Qualfon	More Opportunities	Your Opinion
0 *New Jobs*	**5.18%**	**29,329** *2.7 average hours per employee*	**2.85**
Q1 Target: 270 new jobs	Q1 Target: 5.08% monthly	Q1 Target: 2.5 hours per person	Q1 Target: 3.06+ monthly

View Mission Metric Video at *youtu.be/1xkmDvQ7tP8*. For more company examples of mission metrics, visit *hwaw.com/guideresources*.

2.5 Develop a Communication Plan.

Communication is a strategic component for a mission and values driven company and for advancing a Caring Culture. Here are a few key points we have learned along the way:

- Conduct a Strategic Communication Planning session to prepare your Communication Plan.
- Communicate in person whenever possible (refer to Lencioni's *The Advantage*).
- Deliver the communication in a sincere way.
- Never lose sight of the ultimate goal of the journey.
- Ensure ongoing communication and communication planning

Communication Planning Steps:

1. Develop the message *(WHAT do you want to say?)*
   - What are you doing?
   - Why are you doing it?
   - Where does the CEO journey fit in?
   - What are the Purpose, Mission and Core Values?
   - What is and why have a Caring Team?
   - What is and why have Caring Activities?
2. Determine the audience *(WHO do you want to say it to?)*
   - Employees?
   - Their families?
   - The community?
   - Your customers, vendors, partners?
   - Other stakeholders?

3. Develop a plan on how to share it *(what is the MEDIUM you will use?)*
   - Company wide meeting?
   - Location town halls?
   - Videos?
   - Website?
   - Email?
   - Newsletters?
   - Business Cards?
   - Location monitors?
4. Develop the schedule (WHEN are you going to share it?)
   - Date and time
   - Frequency
5. Develop a plan to measure the effectiveness of the Communication Plan (Did it work as planned?)
   - Implement a simple feedback survey
   - Review plan vs. actual

STAKEHOLDER COMMUNICATION PLAN			
Stakeholder	Communication	Medium	Schedule
Employees			
Caring Team			
Vendors			
Community			
Other Companies			

2.6 Summarize Your Implementation Plan *(who, what, when where?)*

At this point in the journey, your team has identified actions from the Purpose, Mission and Core Values exercise, the Caring Matrix Assessment, the Caring Team, the KPIs and your Communication Plan that need to be captured and tracked as part of an on-going implementation. Summarize all the implementation activities into a plan that is owned by the Vision Team. Identify the person responsible for managing the plan and the process for reviewing the plan.

You can use any format that you are comfortable with or that may be part of an existing process used in your company. The main objective is to be clear on the who, what, when, and where for each activity related to the transformation plan and to ensure that the team is held accountable to following the plan.

ACTION	Who	What	When	Cost
Implement Core Value Survey				
Implement or Improve Caring Activities				
Implement Caring Activity Metrics				
Hand-off to Caring Team				
Execute Communication Plan				
Integrate Metrics				

A Communication Plan should be used for the initial roll out and for on-going communication. Both are equally important to the success of the transformation. If you would like to learn more about how our HWAW companies are communicating this journey, please contact us at *hwaw.com*.

STEP 2 POTENTIAL OBSTACLES

The Vision Team will not commit to the resources needed to implement the plan.

One CFO at a HWAW company pointed out if this initiative is critically important for the CEO and the company, then it needs to be treated in the same way we would treat any other company-level strategic initiative. This means it needs a seat at the table with the other projects and must be managed, provided resources, reported, measured, etc., in the same way. If you are not willing to resource it appropriately, then you are not ready to implement HWAW.

The CEO just wants to go do it without a plan or communication.

We have many examples of companies that have attempted to implement HWAW on their own time and in their own way after reading *The Business Card* book or listening to a HWAW testimony. Some have been very successful and some have not. Since the ultimate purpose of this initiative is greater than any other initiative, the expectations are high and we don't want to see anyone fail. For HWAW, the faster the company can implement, the faster they can begin to create a Caring Company Culture and provide Eternal Value. However, each CEO and company is different and there are many valid reasons for following a customized process that meets the needs of the company. We developed this guide to provide a process you can follow on your own time and in your own way, but at the end of the day it is up to the CEO how you decide to implement it.

The Vision Team does not understand the need for metrics.

Sometimes the Vision Team has a difficult time understanding how to measure caring and behavior. They see it differently than productivity, or quality: things that seem to be easier to measure. It is important that you answer the question: "how do you know if you are fulfilling the

Purpose, Mission and Core Values?" Not just for the ROI output, but also the EternalROI™. We recommend that you don't go to the next step until these metrics are agreed on. They will drive everything.

STEP 2 SUCCESSES

1. "In 2013, we launched the Corporate Chaplain program as part of our efforts to live our Core Values in the workplace. We have seen many positive effects as the Donnelly chaplain provides professional and personal support to our employees and their families. This program helps us to touch our employees in a special way in times of crisis or at other critical junctures in their lives."
   —Martin D. Tighe,
      Founder and Chairman, Donnelly Communications, Inc.

2. "HWAW has been instrumental in helping us implement a Christ centered caring culture with the introduction of Caring Committees throughout our organization. Providing our team members the opportunity to have significance and create eternal value has been critical in deploying our mission and transforming our culture."
   —Brad Thompson, CEO of Columbia Forest Products

3. A HWAW CEO shared this story: "The same salesman that challenged me for wearing my faith on my sleeve, upon entering the chapel for the first time, sarcastically asked me, 'Do people actually use this chapel?' Well, before I could answer, the Master of the Universe sent the answer… the door opened and a welder in full welding gear came into the chapel on his break, went onto his knees and began to pray. I looked at the salesman and smiled, 'I guess people do use it.' Since that day, we have had to clean the carpet many times, as people from all departments visit the chapel to give praise and ask for guidance, bringing their joys and sorrows before 'The True Boss.'"

4. Your answers to each of these questions have to be your own. This story could be seen as an obstacle if the company did not overcome it. For your Purpose, Mission and Core Values, have to be your own. They will not work if you just copy and paste something that sounds good or something a company (even if it is in the same industry) may be using that works for them. At the beginning, some business leaders were so excited to openly share their faith in their company

that they would just copy and paste the Core Values or Mission of Peter's company, Polydeck. We were so excited that they were willing to do this that we did not care. It was a step down the declaration road and that was part of the intent, right? We soon learned that if the answers don't align with the unique DNA of the company or company's leader, they will not work over time. It made it difficult for the existing employees to connect with another company's Purpose, Mission and Core Values, even if they understood and agreed on the ultimate reason for doing this. Here is an example of the company's new values once they developed them from their own family-owned business DNA.

Example of a Core Values based on a HWAW company's DNA

Taylor Made Core Values

Care for our Customers, Team Members
and Horses like they are Family.

Deliver Smiles through Service.

Have Fun while Striving for Excellence.

Always look for a Better Way.

*Taylor Made (taylormadestallions.com), provides a full spectrum
of services for the Thoroughbred Industry.*

STEP 2 COMPANY RESULTS

During the Vision workshop with a CEO of a professional engineering and projects firm, the CEO became very emotional. He could feel the Holy Spirit at work and we could see and hear it in the discussions and interactions of the team. It was difficult to find the right words, select the right Core Values and agree as a team. These were very tough choices to make. The CEO knew he wanted the decisions to represent the company he founded and how they would honor God as a team as they moved forward. He also knew he would have to take a stronger position than he had been to do this right. At one point, he stood up and said, "That's it, I am coming out of the closet for God." From then on, all of the work required in step 2 was led by the Holy Spirit as well as supported by his Caring Team leader and HWAW coach.

Example of Output of Step 2.1

Our Purpose:

Serve God as we find the solutions for Geotechnical challenges, grounded in technical excellence and social responsibility.

Our Core Values:

1. **Passion** – The desire to solve new challenges, the disposition to serve them with love and perseverance and giving more than expected.

2. **Service** – Spontaneously and effectively helping your neighbors to address their needs.

3. **Honesty** – Acting in a clear and transparent manner with truth, justice and humility.

4. **Family** – Collaborating in leveraging our strengths and helping each other to overcome our individual weaknesses in order to reach common goals.

Example of output from Step 2.2

COMPANY RESULTS		
Physical	*Emotional*	*Spiritual*

Employees

Physical	Emotional	Spiritual
• Ping Pong Club • Active Breaks • Health Awareness • Pilates Club • Company Soccer Team • Climbing Wall • Cooking Club • Swimming Club	• Operators School • Alcohol Rehab • Mentor/Coaching Program • Financial Education • Core Value and Behavior Education • Subsidized Medication Program	• Chaplain • Bible Study • Place to Pray • Spiritual Retreats

Families

Physical	Emotional	Spiritual
• Family Celebration • Scholarships • House Repair	• Workshop for Mothers and Children (Building Relationships and Trust) • Psychology • Story Contest for Children	• Chaplain • Annual Worship Appreciation

Community

Physical	Emotional	Spiritual
• Veterans Foundation	• Nursing Home Visits • Foundation for Burn Victims • Heart Foundation	• Foundation of the Holy Cross

Examples of output from Step 2.3

This Committee was elected by the initial management committee for a period of one year 2015 • 2016. Each Member belongs to a different area in the organization.

Committee Mission:

1. Promote the values of work, family and society
2. Give opportunities for improvement to the employees of Geotechnica and their families physically, emotionally and spiritually
3. Spread a culture of support to family members
4. Develop and explore human potential which will allow us to realize goals
5. Support our communities
6. Educate and strengthen our core value behaviors

Examples of output from Step 2.4

ROI INDICATORS	
Financials	• Billing • Profitability
Clients	• Customer Satisfaction • Number of New Clients
Community	• Training Hours • Turnover • Money Invested In Social Related Causes
EternalROI™ INDICATORS	
Souls Touched	• Meaningful one on one conversations between leaders and employees (job and Core Value performance review sessions) • Number of Salvations • Number of personal visits for care and life planning sessions with Chaplain
Organizational Climate	• Employee Satisfaction • Reduction of Accidents
Core Value Strength	• Core Value Survey • Community Service Hours per Employee

Examples of output of Step 2.5

COMMUNICATION PLAN		
Stakeholder	*Communication and Medium*	*Schedule*
Employees	**Email and Mail Campaigns**	+6 times a month
	Intranet Sections with new features	Once a month
	Company Billboard News of caring events	Daily Messages
	Whatsapp Working groups	Daily Messages
	Voice to Voice Contact one by one	Daily Messages
	Meetings Group by area	Weekly
	Messages on Vending	Every 2 Months Approx.
Caring Committee	**Email and Mail Campaigns**	Once a month
	Intranet Sections with new features	Once a month
	Company Billboard News of caring events	Once a month
	Whatsapp Working groups	Daily Messages
	Voice to Voice Contact one by one	Daily Messages
	Meetings of the Caring Committee	2 Times a Month
Community	Presentations with individual groups/organizations	As Identified
	Presentations with many groups/organizations	Once a Year
Suppliers	Website Link	On-going
	Newsletter	Once a Year
	End of Year Message	December

STEP 2 PROCESS CHECK

☐ Purpose, Mission, Core Values and behaviors have been defined

☐ Current company level Caring Activities have been identified

☐ 1–3 Caring Activities that you want to implement or improve at the company level been identified

☐ The implementation plan for these 1–3 initiatives has been defined

☐ The first Caring Team (people, structure, budget) has been identified

☐ The hand-off for the first Caring Team has been planned

☐ The Purpose/Mission Metrics (Company level EternalROI™ and ROI KPIs) have been defined

☐ The Communication Plan has been developed

☐ All decisions and actions have been summarized into an implementation plan — who, what, when, and where?

NOTES

STEP THREE

Cascading Engagement

6

LEADER'S PRAYER

Dear Lord,

Thank You for being with me and my leadership as we have developed, struggled, debated, cried, engaged, and prayed together while developing a transformational plan for our company. My heart (and hopefully, the hearts of most of my Vision Team) is on fire to share my love of You with the rest of the company. We know that some people will be scared, some will be angry, some will be overjoyed, and some may not care at all. As we begin to cascade our Caring Plans throughout the company, we ask that You bless this plan and give us the strength to implement it with respect, excellence, and love in a way that pleases You.

> *"A new command I give you: Love one another. As I have loved you, so you must love one another. By this everyone will know that you are my disciples, if you love one another."*
> JOHN 13:34-35

Please help me to remember that I am not in this alone and I can turn to You at any time for discernment and prayer and that HWAW is here for me, also. In the end, all of the success from this journey is for YOU.

In Your Name,
Amen

1 *Align the Vision Team* — CEO

2 *Create Your Implementation Plan* — VISION TEAM

3 *Cascade Engagement* — CARING TEAM

4 *Live Out His Way at Work* — COMMUNITIES, FAMILIES, & EMPLOYEES

We were working with a HWAW company with over 2,500 employees in 15 locations in North America and Canada that developed a Company Foundation to fund the company-level Caring Activities. They appointed an Executive Director to manage the programs and funding in addition to leading the Caring Team implementation across the company with the help of a HWAW coach. They were implementing a Caring Team within each of the 15 locations that would make local decisions on how to care. She shared this communication with the entire company prior to the hand-off meeting for the first Caring Team.

STEP 3 CASE STUDY

Internal Communication
Feb. 2016

As you may already know I've recently been appointed the Executive Director of our new Columbia Forest Products Foundation. One of the things I'm most proud of as an employee is our generous nature, and how we genuinely care for one another and the communities we live in. …

Caring Committees will be formed at each mill to help shape the programs that will provide support to our employees, their families and our communities. The Committees will be made up of representatives of all shifts and departments at each mill. Initially, Caring Committee members will be appointed by the local Plant Manager and HR Manager. However, future members will be identified from volunteers. Committee members will serve 2-year terms. We will begin rolling the program out at our NC mills during the 1st quarter of 2016.

In preparation for my new duties, a few of us visited several His Way At Work Partner companies that have already installed "Caring Committees." They allowed us to sit in on meetings as they discussed some of the needs of their employees and community civic groups (the identity of the employees requesting assistance are kept anonymous from the Committee Members).

- We watched the groups decide to pay off a past due utility bill for a family because one of the family members had lost their job and the family's income was greatly diminished.
- Another group held a sock and shoe drive to provide low-income families in their communities with new shoes and socks during the winter months.
- We watched as another group planned to provide Thanksgiving meals to needy families in their community.

However, one particular situation sticks out in my mind. An employee had requested a loan to help obtain a mattress, linens and toiletries for a new home. In her letter she stated it was her wish not to sleep on a pallet any longer. She indicated that she would repay the loan, if granted, in 9 months.

It sounded reasonable, and I was sure the group was leaning towards providing those items for her. As we watched this Caring Committee discuss the request, they started to wonder…

if this person was in need of something as basic as a mattress, could she really afford to pay back a loan? Upon further review they learned that this person had been homeless for the last 15 months, but had managed to hold down a full-time job. She had been written up 2 times for missing work without calling in, but that's because she didn't have a phone. All things considered, it was remarkable that she had maintained her employment.

The Caring Committee members weren't satisfied with just honoring her request for a loan, they really cared for her, like a family would do. They determined that given her current income and the new expenses associated with paying for an apartment it was unlikely that she could afford to pay back a loan in 9 months and stay current with her bills. They decided that if she made the 1st two loan payments on time, they would forgive her loan and gift her these items instead. In addition to the mattress set, linens and toiletries she requested, they also planned to provide her with grocery store gift cards so that she could stock her kitchen with food. I don't mind telling you that watching the entire process brought me to tears (yes, I'm a softy). I had a new understanding of what "caring" for one another means. I know we've all heard that "charity starts at home," but most of the time we don't even realize that the people we work with each and every day have basic needs that aren't met. Our Foundation will allow us a way to formally assist our employees, their families and the communities in which we live. We want to make a significant difference in the lives of people. I'm excited to get started in this endeavor and I look forward to working with you all to this end.

Sincerely,

Michele Ford
Executive Director, Columbia Forest Products Foundation

◆ ◆ ◆

By the time you have reached this step, you have educated the Vision Team, defined their roles and responsibilities, and developed the plan for implementing HWAW in your company. The Vision Team plays the most critical initial role in cascading engagement. At this point, you should be able to assume the Vision Team is committed to fulfilling their obligations as we move into Step 3. They will be measured and held accountable in Step 4.

What is Step 3?

Cascading engagement is the key step for ensuring the decisions you have just made on how to genuinely care are integrated into the organization through everything you do. This is how caring becomes a living, breathing part of the organization.

Although we could not find an official definition for cascading engagement in the dictionary, we have defined it as:

> *The act of continually engaging all employees in the His Way at Work process so that it eventually becomes part of one shared culture of caring.*

Why Complete Step 3?

In order to truly cascade engagement, the team must be clear on what this means. Often with new initiatives, you develop a plan, approve the plan and then execute. Every execution is made up of a list of action items to be completed, just like the action items you defined as a result of Step 2. However, how you execute them will determine the overall effectiveness of the initiative. If you are truly committed to this initiative, then you are setting much higher expectations than traditional secular initiatives like Total Quality, Lean, ISO, etc. You are committing to creating Eternal value by living your Purpose and Core Values. This is a BIG deal!

Cascading will not be successful if it is thought of as a single event. It must be thought of as a continual journey that only grows and strengthens over time, like building a relationship. In this case, we are building hundreds and possibly thousands of relationships with each employee, their families, and the community.

STEP 3 PROCESS

There are two unique steps to begin to cascade engagement.

3.1   Complete the Hand-off to the Caring Team

3.2   Institutionalize Caring

We like to think of 3.1 as passing your key message to your initial disciples for caring and 3.2 as how you develop more disciples for caring over time. Although these may seem like simple, straightforward steps, how you execute them will be critical to the success of transforming the culture.

There are four primary groups within the company responsible for cascading engagement. All four are responsible for living the company Purpose, Mission and Core Values and caring for each other.

- The Vision Team (including the CEO)
- The Caring Team
- Direct Line Supervisors
- Employees

As a member of the Vision Team, as shared in Chapter 4, you are responsible for setting the environment for the hand-off meeting and conducting the hand-off meeting according to the plan you developed in Step 2.3.

Roles and Responsibilities of the Vision Team

Role: To help transform the culture of the organization by implementing and living out the HWAW process and to live the HWAW process by being an example to all employees. After all, the Vision Team should model desired behaviors.

Responsibilities:

1. Being a role model to live out the Mission and Core Values
2. Actively participating in the hand-off meeting
3. Supporting and encouraging the members of the Caring Team
4. Promoting participation in Caring Activities to all employees
5. Promoting support for the Caring Team to all supervisors
6. Holding themselves accountable to the implementation plan

Roles and Responsibilities of the Caring Team

As a member of the Caring Team, you are responsible for creating an environment to honor God and providing employees physical, emotional and spiritual assistance in their personal, familial, and community levels through the following objectives:

- **Serving:** The Caring Team's main objective is to serve employees, families and the community.

- **Teambuilding:** Remind employees how they strengthen each other.

- **Role Modeling:** Identify a role model to encourage employees to live the company's Core Values.

- **Delegating:** Caring Activities are driven by employees; the Caring Team represents all employees. They decide which Caring Activities the company should implement, who to help and how much to support each case. Senior executives are discouraged from making the decisions or monitoring allocation.

- **Listening:** "Who needs help?"

As a Caring Team member, you are also responsible for promoting an environment where:

- Core Values and social responsibilities are lived out and experienced in daily operations.

- People are encouraged and given opportunities to improve their workplace, physical health, mental and spiritual growth.

- People trust and support each other in a caring and fun family manner. Don't forget to have FUN.

- People are encouraged to explore and apply their potential to realize their dreams.

- People are involved beyond their daily work duties and actively participate in shaping the corporate culture and supporting their communities.

- All this is done in a non-discriminatory and non-threatening way.

Roles and Responsibilities of Direct Line Supervisors

As a direct supervisor, you are responsible for being a "Mission" Manager in the way you serve the company and the people you serve. This is done by:

- Living the Purpose and Core Values.
- Owning the Purpose and Mission Metrics for your team.
- Supporting your employees that serve as Caring Team members.
- Encouraging your employees to participate on the Caring Team and to support Caring Team activities.
- Personally listening and understanding the needs of your employees and helping them to meet their needs when possible personally or through the Caring Team.

Roles and Responsibilities of Employees

An employee that is not on the Vision Team or Caring Team or a supervisor has the following responsibilities:

- Living the company Purpose and Core Values.
- Caring for each other in daily activities while listening and responding to their needs.
- Participating in Caring Activities.

3.1 Complete the Hand-off to the Caring Team.

Being a part of the hand-off as a Vision Team or a Caring Team member is a special opportunity. You are part of a company that is committed to having a Caring Company culture and you are being asked to help determine how best to invest the company profits in a way that can lead to eternal rewards.

Conducting the Hand-off

This is when you execute the hand-off according to the plan you developed in step 2.3. Once the hand-off is complete, assess how it went. Was everything covered? What did you learn? What feedback did you get?

3.2 Institutionalizing Caring

This involves four areas:

- An engaged and effective Caring Team
- A process for recognizing behaviors that support Core Values
- Engaged and effective Direct Line Supervisors
- Engaged employees who care for each other

Engaged and Effective Caring Team

Institutionalizing caring requires a process for continually understanding employees', their families' and the community's needs. Caring Activities are a means for meeting these needs. Every employee should find at least one activity in the Caring Matrix that meets their needs. If the activities provided do not meet the needs, then why have them? In order to truly meet the needs, the Caring Team (and the direct supervisor, who we will discuss later) has to know them. Refer to the Caring Matrix Assessment in Step 2. The Caring Team should make this a living, breathing document.

What is your process as a Caring Team to continually:

- Understand and assess needs?
- Adjust (eliminate, improve or add) activities to meet the needs?
- Assess the effectiveness of the activities?

How do we know if the Caring Team is in place, functioning and operating under their roles and responsibilities?

- Meetings are taking place on schedule.
- Caring Team members are showing up.
- Decisions are being made (although often difficult).
- Funds are being used according to guidelines.
- Non-Caring Team members within the company know what is happening.
- Employees want to be on the Caring Team.
- New ideas are being generated.
- Meetings are fun and productive.
- Caring Team members are held accountable.
- Actions items are being followed up on.
- The team makes decisions on their own without waiting for senior leadership or manager approval.
- The Caring Team takes action for caring on their own.

Process for Recognizing Behaviors that Support Core Values

One way to help you measure if employees are demonstrating the Core Values is to look for them and recognize them for it. This program can be customized for your company.

COMPANY NAME
Caught You Caring

Help us recognize that special employee who
you have "caught caring" for yourself or others.
Please complete and return this form to HR or the Caring Team box.

∾

Nominee's Name: _____

Department: _____

Please check the value(s) displayed:

☐ **Value 1:** Brief Description of the value

☐ **Value 2:** Brief Description of the value

☐ **Value 3:** Brief Description of the value

☐ **Value 4:** Brief Description of the value

☐ **Value 5:** Brief Description of the value

I recommend this person because:

_____

_____

_____

_____

_____

_____

∾

Your Name: _____

Date: _____

Example Program: Caught You Caring

- If you see someone demonstrating our Core Values or caring for another person, nominate them for a Caught You Caring Award.
- Each nomination must fall under at least one of the values guidelines to be considered. Consider these examples if the values are:
  ▷ Honesty: Did they do the right thing?
  ▷ Integrity: Demonstrate good values?
  ▷ Attitude: Display a positive attitude during adversity?
  ▷ Kindness: Do a good deed?
  ▷ Compassion: Was there for you during a difficult time?
  ▷ Respect: Show consideration for others?
- All nominations are approved through the Caring Team.
- All approved nominations receive recognition determined by location.
- All Caught You Caring recipients will be recognized in a newsletter and mentioned at the "All Employee" monthly meeting.

Engaged and Effective Direct Line Supervisors

Research why employees leave their job or top reasons for not being engaged, and you will consistently find 'relationship with their boss' as the number one reason. Research found on a Harvard Business Review (HBR, 2014) blog shares:

Secrets to Employee Engagement

3 of the top 4 secrets point to the supervisor:

1. Line supervisors, not HR, lead the charge.

2. Supervisors learn how to hold candid dialogues with teams.

3. Supervisors conduct regular pulse checks (short, frequent, anonymous surveys).

One HWAW company recognized the importance of the role of a manager of people in meeting the Mission and Core Value expectations. They viewed the role of a person that manages people as a Mission Leader responsible for being a mentor, a manager and a messenger leading people toward the company's Mission. They are in process of developing profiles, assessments, workshops and courses to help ensure the Mission Leader is being the best they can be to support the Mission and Core Values of the company.

MISSION LEADER

As a Mission Leader, I will lead by example. I will act as a mentor, manager and messenger.

 As a Mentor, I will help each member of my team succeed in their personal and professional goals and work to improve my own skills and expertise.

 As a Manager, I will ensure that each member of my team contributes to meet our responsibilities to the best of our abilities and strive to live the culture of Qualfon as a mission and STRIDES values driven company.

 As a Messenger, I will represent Qualfon in a professional manner and work to creative a positive view of all things that are Qualfon

To learn more about the Mission Leader program at Qualfon, visit qualfon.com.

Recommended expectations of a people leader in a HWAW company:

- Clear understanding of the Purpose, Mission and Core Value expectations and the ability to communicate these expectations to others.
- Actively lives out the Mission and Core Values.
- Ability to develop healthy relationships with their employees by
  - ▷ Creating an open, trusting environment for their employees to work.
  - ▷ Being compassionate and empathetic.
  - ▷ Understanding employee needs.
  - ▷ Supporting professional development for their employees.
  - ▷ Holding employees accountable to the Mission and Core Values in addition to performance standards.
  - ▷ Understanding what non-discriminatory and voluntary mean.

During a workshop with a HWAW company, the CEO told his team that he expected each of them to know if their people need help and that he wanted to know when people needed help. He was holding his people managers responsible for making sure they understood the needs of their team.

We cannot underestimate how important this is in creating a Caring Company Culture. Statistics show the number of unhappy, unengaged employees is high. As the leader, you can play an important role in keeping employees engaged and happy simply by showing you care for them.

Engaged Employees Who Care for Each Other

As you continue to cascade engagement across the organization, the ultimate goal is for employees to care for each other. You do not want to build a culture where caring is expected and demonstrated only from the top down. This is not cascading. It is mandating and this is not sustainable.

A Caught You Caring program helps to encourage employees to care for each other. If you have already decided to implement a similar program in Step 2, then Congratulations! If not, we encourage you to re-think how this type of program may be able to help you even if you customize it to fit your company and culture.

STEP 3 POTENTIAL OBSTACLES

1. We start to implement and get resistance from the Caring Team. The best way to mitigate this is in the preparation and execution of the hand-off process. In other words, take your time and do it right. Remember you will be changing your company culture. This means changing people's hearts and minds. It won't happen overnight. Go back to Step 2 and make sure you have included all the key points in your planning. Then listen and respond honestly.

2. What if we start to implement and get resistance from employees? This will happen, so the CEO and every member of the Vision Team needs to be prepared for it. The best plan to mitigate this is to have the Vision Team and Direct Line Supervisors educated and bought in, along with a good communication plan. Refer to the reality of the 'bell curve'.

3. Some of our employees just want to come to work, do their job and go home and do not want to spend time 'caring for each other.' This may be the way they feel at the start of the process but over time we hope they will begin to see others caring for each other or others caring for them and eventually reciprocate. It takes time and evidence of genuine

caring, but don't give up. If you know those employees, maybe you can ask them why they feel this way and what could you do differently that would matter to them. We find most people do care for people in some way or another even if it is in their own way. So, the more we know people, the better we can integrate and connect the caring.

4. The Caught You Caring program could turn into a way for employees just to get gifts. Similar programs have failed in the past, because the people don't believe the person that was rewarded was worthy of the reward. This can begin to have an impact on the reputation of the program. The Caring Facilitator or Caring Team should have a process check in place to review, approve and track recognitions to help avoid these situations.

5. Our people leaders have been in place for a long time and do not have a healthy relationship with their team or do not support the 'new' Mission and Core Values. We recommend having an assessment in place that includes development plans for each people manager to help them grow in these areas, along with an assessment on how they are living the Core Values and Purpose. However, if they are not interested or unwilling to change, then it is best for both parties that they move on. This should be a proactive part of the exit program.

STEP 3 SUCCESSES

Employee Testimonials

"The company surrounded me at a time of difficulty helping me with my daughter that has osteo-sarcoma, which is bone cancer. The Caring Committee presented an envelope to all the employees in the plant, and everybody pitched in, and it came out to be almost two thousand dollars."

— Jerry, an employee

"We have had several charities come in, and they have all been so wonderful. This whole program has just influenced my heart so much. It has made me a better person."

— An employee

"I've worked with some projects brought up by the Caring Committee like United Way and Christmas in Action, and it's really brought a lot of pride in my own life, and fulfillment knowing that I'm helping those that are in need, and are less fortunate. And it's also brought employees closer together by working together outside the company."
— DANIEL, AN EMPLOYEE

Find these testimonies and more at *hwaw.com/guideresources*.

Developing your people IS a Caring Activity.

A Chief Mission Officer for another company implementing HWAW was in a meeting with the HR leader about a new feedback program they would be teaching all managers. As she listened to the program she said, "If I am one of the people that will be getting the feedback, I am scared. I don't want to go into this session because it sounds like it is built to only talk about what you have done wrong. Giving feedback as part of the feedback program is a Caring Activity that should be done out of love. We want to help our employees grow and develop and be the best they can be for themselves and for the company." Her main point was a feedback program should be seen as a Caring Activity and should be seen as an act of love, not something to be afraid. If you have a feedback program in place, we encourage you to understand if the program is implemented out of love or is it an activity your employees fear?

If the employee is not doing well or not meeting performance expectations, then this does need to be addressed. Even in a caring culture, it is important that we expect excellence and we cannot go soft on this and still run a productive company. But we can speak with them in a way that they know we are having this conversation because we care. In order to have really good feedback sessions, we have to be able to give them with mercy, love, and truth. This implies that the manager cares for their employee and the employee cares for and trusts their manager. This kind of trust must be earned. It takes time.

Caring takes place even when the boss is gone.

At one HWAW company, the Caring Team Leader and the CEO were out of the country when a temporary employee broke his leg. The employee had only been with the company for a few months. Without any directive from above, his fellow employees, supervisor, the chaplain and others who had not even had the chance to meet him yet showed up at the hospital to visit and let him know they cared. They even started collecting money to help him with the bills (because the Benevolence Fund approved in the company only applied to employees who had worked there for at least 6 months). After learning of this story once the Caring Leader and CEO returned, they were filled with joy to hear that employees were caring for each other outside of work on their own time, without being asked. This is a sign of a Caring Company Culture.

STEP 3 COMPANY RESULTS

We showed up for the first Caring Team hand-off meeting being held at Corporate Headquarters. The CEO, Foundation Director, Vision Team, location Vision Team and new Caring Team members for 2 locations were in attendance. Some of the Caring Team members had worked for this company for 30+ years and had never been at the headquarters. The Foundation director did a wonderful job making people feel special and setting the environment.

The CEO started the meeting with his own story of why he wanted to implement HWAW in the company. He said, "For those of you that know me, I wear my faith on my sleeve. I will not impose it on you, but you know how I feel. Before I retire, I want to make a significant impact on lives inside our company, with your families and the community by caring for you like He did."

At the end of the hand-off meeting, we asked the new Caring Team members how they felt about what was going on and what they were being asked to do. Here is some of the feedback:

- Good project, we'll all be blessed.
- Will make our company stronger.
- Good thing, a lot of people need help.
- Positive things, here. Very good things, morale-wise.
- May improve the quality of our employees.
- Will bring more unity, people working together.
- Great team, with big hearts and dedication.
- Get serious and show up.

- I love it. There'll be things I'll never forget.
- Some people may come to the Lord on this.
- It's a great thing, glad to be a part of it.
- I'm glad the company is going in this direction.
- I'm thrilled! Employees will be more dedicated.
- I'm super-psyched! Let's go!
- We'll see things we normally would not have.
- We'll grow as individuals and inspire others.
- Our product quality will improve.
- Our customers will see this in us.
- When people in the community find out, they are going to want to work here.
- It's going to help me a whole lot.
- This is a platform to take things to a whole new level.
- I'm looking forward to it.
- There will be emotional, tough decisions to be made, but we have solid teams.

One of the Vision Team members stressed how important it is to cultivate the Vision Team by the activities in Step 1. This allowed them to have time to learn and see how other companies were implementing Caring Teams so they could better support the hand-off and the new Caring Team. This is especially important for a company that has multiple operating locations each with their own Caring Team.

STEP 3 PROCESS CHECK

☐ The hand-off to the Caring Team is complete.

☐ Signs of institutionalizing caring throughout the company
are evident.

☐ Feedback from the Caring Team is being collected, reviewed,
and recognized.

☐ Caring Team fears, hesitancies, and questions are being addressed.

NOTES

STEP FOUR

Living Out His Way at Work

7

LEADER'S PRAYER

Dear Lord,

Thank You for Your many blessings as we have started to cascade engagement through our Caring Teams and Caring Activities. Thank You for watching over each Caring Team member as one of your sheep and help them to watch for lost sheep through their caring of other employees, their families, and the community.

Please help me and our teams to grow and lead as a servant, like Jesus did for You. In order to live out HWAW, we know we must be responsive to the needs of those we have asked to act according to the Purpose, Mission and Core Values. Give us the strength, courage and faithfulness to stay focused on our purpose to serve You in hopes of creating Eternal Value.

> *"Therefore, as God's chosen people, holy and dearly loved, clothe yourselves with compassion, kindness, humility, gentleness and patience."*
> COLOSSIANS 3:12

Please help me to remember that I am not in this alone and I can turn to You at any time for discernment and prayer and that HWAW is here for me also. In the end, all of the success from this journey is for YOU.

In Your Name,
Amen

1 *Align the Vision Team* — CEO

2 *Create Your Implementation Plan* — VISION TEAM

3 *Cascade Engagement* — CARING TEAM

4 *Live Out His Way at Work* — COMMUNITIES, FAMILIES, & EMPLOYEES

Again, we have been blessed to work very closely with another HWAW company in the Business Process Outsourcing industry where the founder actually honored God by consecrating his company to God. Talk about jumping and truly integrating purpose into the company. Learn more about consecrating your company at *hwaw.com/guideresources*.

◆ ◆ ◆

What is Step 4:

This step includes how to integrate your Caring Strategy with other critical company strategies in a sustainable way.

4.1 Serve the Purpose

4.2 Integrate Your Caring

4.3 Review and Adjust

4.4 Share Your Learnings

Why complete Step 4?

This is the step to ensure all the work you have done so far to transform your company culture will last. If we stop now, your Caring Strategy will just be another passing initiative, ultimately not fulfilling your Purpose and Mission to honor God.

How to complete Step 4

Does your company culture look like a Caring Company Culture? At the beginning of Chapter 2, we shared a little on what a Caring Company Culture looks like in action. Here were a few of the examples. Does this look like your company culture?

- ☐ Environment of trust because everyone is focused on the company's Purpose and Mission, not individual needs.
- ☐ Employees at all levels genuinely care for each other in daily actions.
- ☐ Employees are aware of the needs of each other.
- ☐ Employees are motivated, engaged and willing to go above and beyond for the company because they know the company will do the same for them.
- ☐ Leaders are servant leaders, not self-serving leaders.
- ☐ Employees openly demonstrate the company's Core Values through their behaviors because they are aware of them, they align with their own, and they want to live them even if they were not asked.
- ☐ Purpose, Mission and Core Values are a common language.
- ☐ Team members welcome prayer together even if they are not all Christian.
- ☐ Team members want to pray for each other even if they are not all Christian.
- ☐ Team members are there when you need them.
- ☐ When you want to learn something new or change paths, you have support to do so.
- ☐ When you mess up, you are forgiven.
- ☐ Excellence is expected.
- ☐ When terminations are required, the person is treated with dignity.
- ☐ People want to work for this company.
- ☐ People don't want to leave the company unless it is for personal reasons or other opportunities for growth.
- ☐ When people leave for personal reasons or opportunities for growth, they are supported and encouraged.
- ☐ Employees care for each other even when the boss is out.
- ☐ Employees say yes to overtime not for the money, but to help the company.
- ☐ Employees are willing to sacrifice pay in the bad times to help the company.

☐ Employees look for ways to be good stewards for the company.

☐ There is healthy focus on safety within the company and for each other.

Do any of these look familiar in your company culture? In Step 4, we will review the key steps to ensure you are living out HWAW.

STEP 4 PROCESS

4.1 Serve Serve the Purpose

When we began to develop our HWAW process, we shared it with many experts and were directed to Lead Like Jesus, co-founded by Ken Blanchard and Phil Hodges. Following their concepts of Jesus-like leadership, we realized it was time to "turn the pyramid upside down." In Step 4, the leader has become the servant of the vision, serving the people they lead. The purpose of the CEO and the Vision Team is to be responsive to the needs of their people who are being asked to respond according to the Purpose, Mission, Values and Caring Metrics set in Steps 1-3.

In a HWAH company, servant leadership starts with the Purpose, Mission and Core Values and is lived out with a servant heart that helps people live according to the purpose, mission and Core Values.

SERVANT LEADERSHIP MODEL

4 Live out His Way at Work

3 Cascade Engagement

2 Create Your Implementation Plan

1 Align the Vision Team

According to Ken Blanchard, Phil Hodges and Phyllis Hendry in Lead Like Jesus Revisited, their most recent work, this leadership model involves:

1. Setting your Purpose.
2. Developing a Compelling Vision.
3. Defining Your Picture of the Future.
4. Identifying and Prioritizing Values.
5. Communicating and Testing for Understanding.
6. Inverting the pyramid to serve those who are responding to others
7. Showing respect for everyone.
8. Highlighting the growth and development of people as an important part of changing the culture.

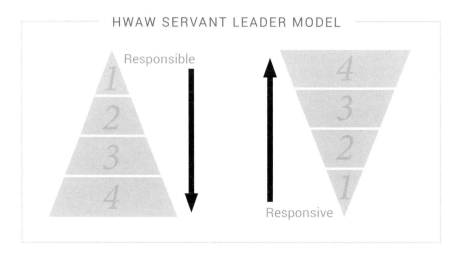

4.2 Integrate Your Caring

In a traditional company, there is usually a Vision or Mission, measures, processes for collecting feedback, reviewing measures, and adjusting plans for the key areas of the company like Manufacturing, Finance, HR and Sales. All activities (hiring, meetings, performance reviews, training, etc.) are focused on being successful in these areas to ultimately produce ROI. Core Values may be defined, but they are often developed based on what is needed to make money, not on Christian values.

Some companies may say they want a Caring Company Culture, but manage it 'on the side' and it truly never has a seat at the executive table with Finance, Manufacturing, Sales and HR. When this happens, you may generate ROI and some eternal impact from trying to live the Core Values but you will not have long term, sustainable EternalROI™. Caring decisions will always be at the bottom of the priority list and will, over time, fade. We have heard many executive team members say "yes, we have Core Values — I can't remember what they are but they are on the wall somewhere" or "yes, we care about our people but making money comes first."

To live out HWAW, your Caring Strategy must have a place at the table and be integrated into all aspects of the organization. The measures and goals you use for monitoring your Caring Strategy must be treated and reviewed the same way as your traditional ROI measures and goals (sales, margin, profit, on-time delivery, productivity, turnover, etc.). Once they are integrated as one, you will begin to see if you are achieving the EternalROI™ results.

Integrating your Caring Strategy includes integrating your measures and a process for collecting feedback. We will cover reviewing and adjusting in Step 4.3. At this point, you should be able to answer the following questions:

1. How have you integrated your EternalROI™ measures?
2. What is your process for collecting feedback?

STEP 4 \ 135

Once the measures and process for collecting feedback are integrated, make sure there is a healthy process for reviewing the feedback and adjusting the plan as needed.

What is the data telling you about how well you are:

- Living your Purpose and Mission?
- Living your Core Values?
- Demonstrating the behaviors identified?
- Meeting the Caring Team mission?
- Leading with a servant's heart?
- Caring for each other — not just from the top down?
- Working as a Vision Team?
- Working as a Caring Team?
- Communicating the journey?

How are you adjusting the plan based on what you are learning?

Use your measures for continuous improvement in the HWAW process

Just collecting and reviewing data will not take you further in this journey if there are no plans to take action as a result of the data. It is important to have a process for identifying and understanding the gaps and determining potential plans for improvement. There are several ways to approach the gaps:

1. As part of an on-going review process
2. As a specific "process improvement" project
3. As part of an annual review of your strategic plan
4. As part of an "open environment" feedback process

Example 1: Weekly Survey Questions
One CEO of a HWAW company, named Mike, sends out a regular weekly survey to all employees with one question regarding how the company is doing to live their Mission. This survey is called, "You Matter To Mike" and each week the question is different. Questions include:

- Do my managers strive to live the values of Qualfon?
- Would you recommend working at Qualfon to a friend or family member?
- Do people care about each other at Qualfon?
- Am I offered training or development opportunities to further myself professionally?

They diligently track the results by location and department to identify where they have opportunities to grow and improve their caring throughout the company and implement plans to help improve. To learn more about this survey and other company surveys available, visit *hwaw.com/guideresources*.

Example 2: Caring Team Process Improvement (PI) Project
A HWAW company held a strategic review with their Caring Team after having the team in place for about 6 years. The purpose was to help the Caring Team identify ways to improve the Caring Activities and the processes for implementing the Caring Activities. The team identified they were missing a robust way to understand and capture employee needs. Even though they had positives results meeting needs in the past, they often missed an important need of an employee or family because they did not know there was a need. They engaged their Manufacturing Process Improvement team to help them understand how to do this in a systematic way to ensure no one fell through the cracks.

EXAMPLE OF COMPANY PI CARING PROJECT

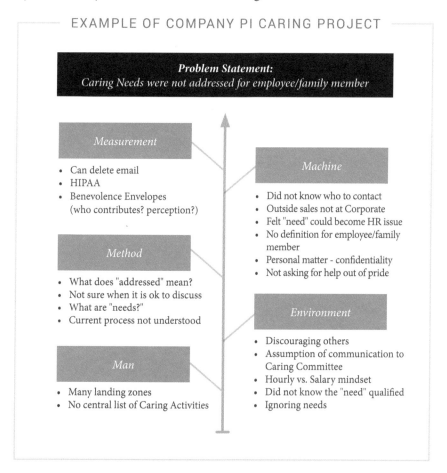

Problem Statement:
Caring Needs were not addressed for employee/family member

Measurement
- Can delete email
- HIPAA
- Benevolence Envelopes (who contributes? perception?)

Machine
- Did not know who to contact
- Outside sales not at Corporate
- Felt "need" could become HR issue
- No definition for employee/family member
- Personal matter - confidentiality
- Not asking for help out of pride

Method
- What does "addressed" mean?
- Not sure when it is ok to discuss
- What are "needs?"
- Current process not understood

Environment
- Discouraging others
- Assumption of communication to Caring Committee
- Hourly vs. Salary mindset
- Did not know the "need" qualified
- Ignoring needs

Man
- Many landing zones
- No central list of Caring Activities

Example 3: Annual Strategic Planning Review

A HWAW company held a review with the Caring Team, Caring Leader, CEO and members of the Vision Team after having a Caring Team in place for 6 years. The purpose of the exercise was to see if they were still on track the original Caring Strategic Plan, Mission and objectives and were there any major changes that needed to take place to continue to improve the Caring Culture. We recommend that companies do not wait 6 years, but implement more frequent reviews (e.g. annually).

Example 4: Open Environment Feedback Process

A company may choose to have a system where employees can provide feedback at any time about the caring programs and caring culture. They may set this up to flow through the Caring Team, management or just through open drop boxes or email. The point here is to provide an environment where people feel comfortable not just giving feedback, but also suggestions on how to take action to adjust the plans.

We have found time after time that the level of organizational health determines the success rate of a HWAW company. If you have low engagement scores due to lack of trust, bad leadership, bad communication, etc. this will be very difficult. How can employees believe you truly want to create a Caring Company Culture if you have these behaviors in place? We know there is no company with perfect organizational health, but a company should know where they stand and have active plans to continue to grow and improve their organizational health.

How is your organizational health?

At a minimum, we recommend the CEO, Vision Team, and site team start by reading *The Advantage*, by Patrick Lencioni or by reviewing the concept of organizational health offered at *tablegroup.com/oh*.

(Graph reprinted with permission from the Table Group).

Reviewing and adjusting to meet your employee needs

During a discussion with a HWAW company, a CEO talked openly about the importance of understanding employees' needs to ensure the Caring Activities are effective. The CEO shared this story, "We were going on mission trips outside of our town to help people build or re-build their homes that were in very bad shape. We felt good about our work but soon realized we had many employees in the company that had houses in the very same shape. Although we still offer mission experiences, we offered a new Caring Activity to help employees inside our own mission field."

Another company implemented a House Repair fund where employees would go help other employees repair their homes. After reviewing the results of this Caring Activity, the data showed there was very little participation in the activity. When the team started to learn why, they found out many people were embarrassed to have someone from the company see the state their house was in, so did not ask for help. The team changed the program to outsource the help and the involvement in the House Repair Fund immediately increased.

After reviewing the results of the annual engagement survey and seeing a drop in the answer to their Core Value, honesty, the company was very concerned. They began to hold round table discussions to learn more about what was causing the drop. They soon learned it was because the company had been asking some employees to consistently work overtime to meet an increase in demand after they had committed to them that the extra time was not required. Because of this, the employees felt like their supervisors were not being honest when communicating the schedule. Although it takes time to add capacity, the company immediately made some changes to try and minimize the situation.

4.4 Share Your Lessons

Once you are implementing Steps 1–4, the most valuable way of living HWAW and building on your success is to share your lessons. There are several ways to do this:

- Include the successes and failures in your internal communications.
- Connect with other CEOs through local networks like C12, Christian Chamber of Commerce, FCCI, and Legatus.
- Connect with other CEOs through HWAW.

- Connect with other Caring Team Leaders through HWAW.
- Sign up for continued education and sharing through HWAW.

Examples of how HWAW connects companies today:

1. Schedules visits for new Caring Teams to observe existing Caring Teams.
2. Provides Caring Team Leaders with lists of Caring Activities and team guidelines.
3. Provides new HWAW companies with a vast library of examples from existing HWAW companies.
4. Connects CEOs with HWAW CEOs before the journey even starts, creating a mentor for the entire journey.
5. Connects Caring Team Leaders with other Caring Team Leaders so they can reach out directly to one another, building on-going learning relationships.
6. Shares success and failure stories across companies.

One Size does not fit all

A CEO of a small HWAW company was sharing an update with us on how his Caring Team and Caring Activities were going. He had started the journey by implementing many of the same Caring Activities that Polydeck did, but soon found several of them did not work for his company. This helped him to realize it is ok to take the time to find the Caring Activities that meet the needs of your company — that they can and will look different in each company. Instead of giving up, they simply decided to eliminate the ones that were not working and look for new ones that would be more effective for caring for his employees. By him sharing this with us, it allows us to share the message with other companies at the beginning when they are first determining which Caring Activities are right for them.

Connecting CEOs

HWAW was working with a new company and the CEO still had some doubts about implementation in his company. We connected him with a HWAW CEO of a company in the same industry (they were actually competitors) to share his successes and failures along the journey. It was the start of a great relationship and the new company has made much progress on their own journey.

STEP 4 POTENTIAL OBSTACLES

1. The metric results indicate you have a gap or a roadblock with a specific person or team (like the CEO, the Vision Team, the HR leader, etc.) This is why it is so important to integrate the Caring Strategy so that it does have a seat next to the other company initiatives. By doing so, it should be treated just like it would if the traditional metrics show a performance problem or financial problem linked to a certain person or area. Now if the company is not currently addressing these things in other areas, then we suggest you may want to start with other assessments before implementing HWAW. Depending on the root cause, you may use a true 360 (that incorporates the Core Values and other key leadership traits for your organization), *The 5 Dysfunctions of a Team* or *The Advantage* survey.

2. The company acquires another company. If you have made it to Step 4 and are in the situation where you acquire or merge with new employees, it could be an obstacle if you do not have a strategy for integrating your current Purpose, Core Values, Caring Strategy with the new acquisition. We recommend managing the situation like all other aspects of an acquisition from the beginning (including the due diligence step when you are making a decision to acquire or not). You should know what the Purpose, Core Values and Caring Strategy (or lack of) looks like for the company you are looking to acquire and how much of a gap there is between cultures before making the decision.

STEP 4 SUCCESSES

1. The Caring Strategy and metrics receive the same attention as the financial plan. In the past, the topic of caring rarely came up in the monthly leadership meeting and even when it was on the agenda, it was random and often pushed to the end of the meeting. Now the company spends as much time on the Caring Strategy as it does on the financial strategy. It is first on the agenda and is never skipped.

2. There are trends in the EternalROI™ KPIs. Now that the company is reviewing the metrics in the leadership review, they are able to see positive trends to know where Caring Activities and genuine caring are working and where they are not so they can take action quickly to understand and improve.

3. The Vision Team is stronger. After going through the 4 steps together, including team and organizational assessments, the team is stronger. They are able to speak more openly with truth and love and to make decisions and priorities driven by the Purpose, Mission and Core Value behaviors.

STEP 4 COMPANY RESULTS

Qualfon is an excellent example of truly integrating the Caring Strategy into the Mission of their company. Here are some of ways they have done this:

- Consecrated the Company.
- Established a Mission Office.
- Developed Mission Metrics that are always in front of the employees.
- Held all leaders responsible for the Mission Metrics.
- Integrated the Mission, Core Values and behaviors into the required education.
- Created a Qualfon Univeristy to provide the education to support the Mission.
- Developed a bi-monthly survey from the CEO to the employees to measure how well they are living their Mission and Core Value behavior.
- Constantly review the results from their survey to learn where they can improve.

STEP 4 PROCESS CHECK

☐ A process to know how well you are serving the Purpose is in place and is sustainable.

☐ Your Caring Strategy has been integrated with the other key company initiatives, including the leadership review process of key metrics.

☐ A process for reviewing the results and identifying improvement plans is in place and is sustainable.

☐ A process for monitoring Team and Organizational health is in place and is sustainable.

☐ A proactive process is in place to share the lessons (both positive and negative) internally and externally with other HWAW companies.

NOTES

SUMMARY

8

ENDING PRAYER

Dear Lord,

I am so thankful that You changed my heart so that I would be willing to listen to You and JUMP! In truth and love, as You already know, it has not been easy. There have been some beautiful moments and there have been some very, very, very difficult times. Thank You for challenging me and testing my faith. Thank You for giving me resources to help me through it like my Bible, my chapel, my prayer, my spiritual advisor, my HWAW coach, my church and my HWAW CEO mentor. I can't say I understand all of the challenges I have been through but I do know that if this is Your will, You will give me the strength and courage to pass through them.

> *"And let us run with perseverance the race marked out for us, fixing our eyes on Jesus."*
> HEBREWS 12:1-2

At the end of my every day, this is not about me but about how I can help get my employees to heaven. Please give me the strength to remember my purpose as a leader during this journey.

In Your Name,
Amen

You should be seeing beautiful, Christ-led change in yourself, the Vision Team, and the employees creating change in the culture. Block off some time with the stakeholders identified in your communication plan to ask about the culture when you started vs the culture. Then just listen.

Hopefully what you hear will be worth the Jump!

◆ ◆ ◆

Ask each of the following groups to answer the questions on the following page. Spend time reviewing the answers together.

- CEO
- Vision Team
- Caring/Mission or Foundation Leader
- Caring Team member
- Location Leaders
- Employees
- Community members
- Customers
- Suppliers

Recap

Think about and share answers to the following questions now that the process has been implemented:

What is different for you personally and why?

_____

_____

_____

What is different in your work and why?

_____

_____

_____

What is your relationship with Christ and why?

_____

_____

_____

What is different in how you speak and respond to people and why?

_____

_____

_____

What is different in how you make decisions and why?

_____

_____

_____

What is different in how you work together and why?

_____

_____

_____

What is the impact on our ROI?

_____

_____

_____

What is the single greatest change?

_____

_____

_____

What is the single most difficult task going through this journey?

_____

_____

_____

NOTES

THE HIS WAY AT WORK PROCESS

The HWAW process is a journey for everyone in the company. It must start first with the CEO, then the Vision Team and a plan, then with cascading engagement through caring leaders, the Caring Team, Caring Activities and caring employees. Once caring for each other is a genuine part of the culture, you will see the fruits of using your ROI to create EternalROI™, ultimately helping you to accomplish your purpose to honor God.

STEP TWO

Step Two:

CREATE A
TRANSFORMATION
PLAN

STEP ONE

Step One:

ALIGN THE
LEADERSHIP
TEAM

THE BEGINNING

The Beginning:

START
WITH A CEO
AND A PURPOSE

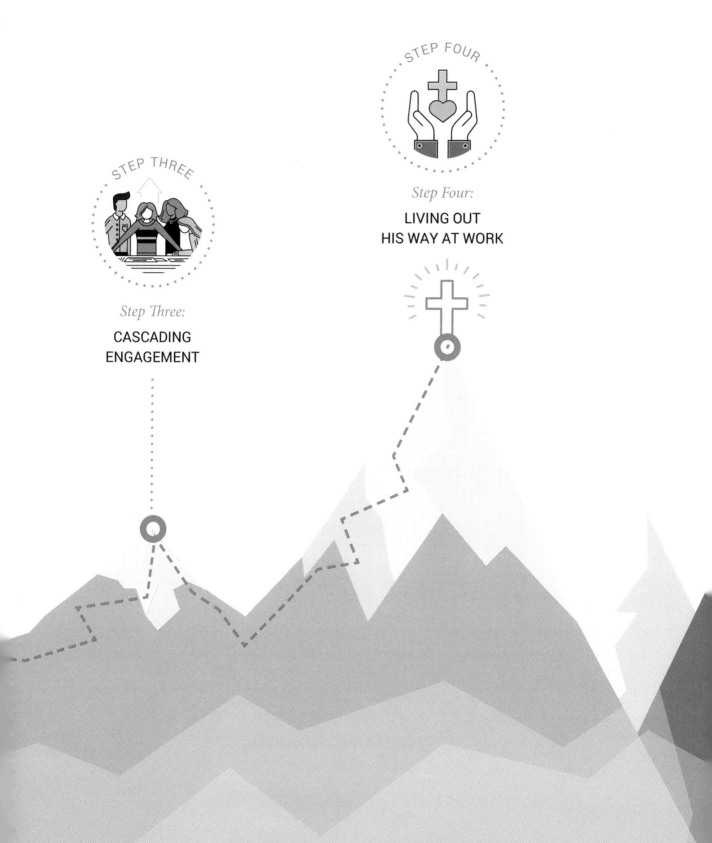

Step Three:

CASCADING
ENGAGEMENT

Step Four:

LIVING OUT
HIS WAY AT WORK

APPENDIX

RESOURCES

HIS WAY AT WORK
A: 1790 Dewberry Road
Spartanburg, SC 29307
P: (866) 570-1229
W: hwaw.com

THE TABLE GROUP, INC.
A: 250 Lafayette Circle, Suite 300
Lafayette, CA 94549
P: (925) 299-9700
F: (925) 299-9708
W: tablegroup.com

C12 GROUP
A: 13403 George Road
San Antonio, TX 78230
P: (210) 767-6200
F: (210) 767-6200
W: c12group.com

CORPORATE CHAPLAINS OF AMERICA
A: 1300 Corporate Chaplain Dr.
Wake Forest, NC 27587
P: (919) 570-0700
W: chaplain.org

LEAD LIKE JESUS
A: 198 White Star Point
Spartanburg, SC 29301
P: (800) 383-6890
W: leadlikejesus.com

HOW TO JOIN HWAW

His Way At Work is called to be a family of business leaders, a meeting place where we exchange how God is putting in each of our hearts that we can follow Him in our day to day jobs. We are a reservoir of Christian workplace-related Best Practices. We are an Association of like-hearted and like-minded business leaders who are taking charge and responsibility to shape the world for the best through our day to day businesses with a long term vision of humanity guided by the Universal teachings that Christ and the Church have shared with us.

You can join His Way At Work at a level that meets your needs from an observer to becoming an active speaker sharing both your personal and your business leader journeys. As a Member we have several yearly suggested contribution brackets depending on the number of employees in your organization.

Your Membership will contribute toward the never ending building of this Ministry but will also give you access to:

- Member's Directory
- Content
- Caring Activities Library
- Monthly newsletter including interviews and case studies which will inspire and help the business leaders on their business transformation journey
- Videos
- Articles, whitepapers and other recommended readings
- Other, like Job Descriptions for Caring Team Members, etc.
- Webinars
- Caring Manager Forums
- Annual Conference
- Coaching Services as needed
- CEO Mentoring Program

To become a member you can:
Sign up at *hwaw.com* or call our toll free number: 1-866-570-1229

ACKNOWLEDGEMENTS

Special Thanks:

Very special thanks go to Kelly Slate, His Way At Work's Operations and Learning Director and "wind beneath the wings" for creating this guide. She has used her 20 years experience in the corporate world and her God-given talents to turn the His Way at Work journey into a replicable process that companies can follow and adapt to meet their own caring needs to ultimately create Eternal Value. She continues to improve and update our processes and this guide as His Way At Work continues to share and grow the number of companies we are blessed to work with in one way or another.

- Scott Gajewsky
  *Founding Executive Director
  and Coach of HWAW*

- Amy Heitt
  The Table Group

- Patrick Lencioni
  The Table Group

- Mark Cress
  *Founder of Corporate
  Chaplains of America*

- Mike Sharrow
  C12 CEO

- Jeff Hillis
  *Chairman of Corporate
  Chaplain of America*

- Jody Armstrong
  His Way at Work Coach

- Sheila Burroughs
  His Way at Work Coach

- Hans Tanner
  True North Consulting

- Susan Ballantyne
  Executive Assistance, Polydeck

- Grant Edwards
  C12 Group Leader

Companies that have supported or implemented His Way at Work:

- Aceites-Essencefleur
- ACR Supply
- ADDIE Solutions
- Agrobetania S.A.
- Alpha & Omega Group
- American Recycling of
  West North Carolina

- Autofletes Chihuahua *(AFC)*
- Bepensa
- Blue Ridge Cabinet Works
- Columbia Forest Products
- Consultores en Riesgos
  y Beneficios
- Covintec *(Qualypanel SA de CV)*

- Custom Forest Products
- Custom Pallet *(now Kamps Pallets)*
- Danny Herman Trucking
- Donnelly Communications, Inc.
- El Jarocho Foods
- Geotecnia y Cimentaciones
- Grace Management Group
- Green Textile
- Grupo GAP
- Guest & Brady
- Hampton Farms
- Health First Urgent & Primary Care
- Hipp Engineering & Consulting
- House of Raeford Farms
- House-Autry Mills
- Jump Start Ministries
- McAlister-Smith Funeral Home
- MN del Golfo
- Norsan Group/Prime Meats, LLC
- Oakbrook Preparatory School
- Oaklawn Academy
- Oilmens Equipment Corp
- oobe *(Out of Bible Experience)*
- Outsourcing, S.A.
- Paragon Clinical
- Pedelta
- Polydeck Screen Corp.
- Polymer-Specialties
- Premier Physical Therapy
- PreVeo
- PrintTek

- Providence Healthcare
- Qualfon
- Real Resorts *(Playa Hotels & Resorts)*
- Renfrow Brothers
- Riva Precision Mfg
- Riverside Veterinary Hospital
- RSN Promotionals
- Southside Barbershop
- Spartan Felt
- Spartanburg Regional Healthcare
- St Mary's Catholic School
- St. Simon & St. Jude Catholic Church
- Sturm & Cont, P.A.
- Sun Surveillance, Inc.
- Sunbelt USA
- Synchro
- Taylor Made Farms
- The Fisher-Barton Group
- Tillotson Enterprises, Inc.
- Tolteca Foods
- Total Comfort Solutions
- Trisure
- TruePresence
- Valley Rubber, LLC
- Visiting Angels
- Visual South Inc.
- Witherspoon Rose Culture *(Pike Enterprises, Inc.)*
- Wolverine Coatings, Corp.

GLOSSARY OF TERMS

Behaviors: The way in which one acts or conducts oneself, especially toward others.

Caring Activity: An activity sponsored by the organization that demonstrates living out Core Values through physical, emotional and/or spiritual caring for employees, families and/or communities.

Caring Company Culture: When a company is living with Christian Core Values that promote genuine caring for employees, their families, and the communities they live in and work at (customers, vendors, suppliers) through caring activities. As genuine caring is demonstrated, Eternal Value (EternalROI™) is created and thus morale, engagement and productivity grow. These also lead to increased profits as a byproduct which is in turn re invested in caring activities, thus creating a virtuous cycle of ROI–EternalROI™.

Caring Matrix: Our unique tool for helping companies love their employees, families and community like their neighbors by providing Caring Activities to not only meet physical and emotional needs but also, and ultimately most importantly: spiritual needs.

Caring Team: A team comprised of employees across the company that helps to cascade engagement throughout the organization by using the Caring Matrix and Caring activities.

Cascade Engagement: The act of continually engaging all associates in the HWAW process so that eventually becomes part of one shared culture of caring.

Caught You Caring: A program that allows employees to recognize each other when they demonstrate examples of the core value behaviors for each other.

CEO: The person or persons that are the ultimate decision maker(s) in the organization other than a board. The actual title may be Company Owner, COO, President or Partner.

CEO Journey: A term used to help the CEO understand where they are along their journey of influencing and declaring with the ultimate goal of providing EternalROI™.

Core Values: The few (3–4) key values by which we live our life, how we behave. Our true Core Values are the principles we use to guide us in our decisions, and help us in those crossroads of life where we might be pulled in opposing directions.

EternalROI™: A term used by His Way at Work to think about how you would measure the potential Eternal value gained by investing in a Caring Company Culture.

Eternal Value: The things in life that will remain valuable forever such as your relationship with God and the people you reach through caring and sharing like Jesus taught us.

HWAW: A non-profit inspiring and helping business leaders to improve their workplace by having God at the center and caring for people as He did, to create Eternal value.

HWAW 4 Step Process: The HWAW process for implementing a Caring Company Culture.

Mission: A one-sentence statement describing what the organization does day to day and used is to help guide decisions about priorities, actions, and responsibilities.

Mission Manager: A manager of people responsible for meeting the mission and core value expectations of the company.

Purpose: The ultimate reason for being that transcends over time.

ROI: A common performance measure used by company leaders to measure the gain or loss generated on an investment relative to the amount of money invested. ROI is usually expressed as a percentage and is typically used for personal financial decisions, to compare a company's profitability or to compare the efficiency of different investments.

Transformation Leader: The person responsible for leading the HWAW implementation within the company. This can be the CEO or someone designated like a Caring Facilitator or HR leader.

Vision Team: The core Leadership Team responsible for helping the CEP shape the company culture by implementing HWAW.

THE IMPORTANCE OF PEER GROUPS

From Peter Feissle

If you are serious about honoring God through the business, showing the love of Christ to your people and navigating challenges along the way, it's critical you don't go about it alone. For years I have found great value in having a group of peers I meet with regularly who are also running businesses with an eternal perspective, to encourage me, challenge me, and hold me accountable. The largest group like this is The C12 Group which have CEO peer advisory groups in cities all over the country. There are other group options as well. What is so vital is that you find a group of peers who are like-minded, not only wrestling with the challenges of being the leader of a company, but the shared perspective of going about it in this uniquely Christ-centered way. You'll be surprised how peer groups can help you actually scale your business and leadership in ways that increases the capacity for greater ministry throughput. Every CEO should be in a peer group, and Christian CEOs should find fellow believers and an intentional format to help maximize the potential each leader and company has in ROI and EternalROI™ terms!

Although HWAW enjoys a strategic partnership with the C12 Group, there are other peer groups available. Here are a few:

- Convene
- FCCI
- Truth@Work
- Pinnacle Forum
- CEO Forum

102 MINISTRY IDEAS FOR YOUR BUSINESS

Looking for practical ways to incorporate ministry into your business?
Here is a list of proven ideas you and your team can implement!

EMPLOYEE AND STAFF MINISTRY

1. Establish written biblical principles and values as clarifying priorities for your firm.

2. Contract to provide professional, third party chaplain care for your employees (Marketplace Chaplains USA).

3. Establish a weekly prayer time and/or Bible study during lunch or off-hours.

4. Create an internal, shareable document for company prayer requests to reference and update during staff meetings.

5. Sponsor the cost of Christ-centered seminars and webinars for your employees.

6. Create an online library of biblical resources.

7. Subscribe to a service such as RightNow Media, which offers free Bible studies and relevant resources on family/life topics.

8. Create an internal, online sign-up for employees to help each other with personal tasks to promote caring for one another.

9. When employees have surgeries, births, or other life-changing events, use an online sign-up program for others to take them a meal.

10. Offer free protective software for parents who wish to safeguard their personal computers and phones.

11. Provide tools for stewardship of their money, such as *mint.com* or Everydollar, and budgeting courses via Financial Peace University, Dave Ramsey, Crown Financial or similar services.

12. Offer payroll auto-deductions, so people can easily donate to ministries of their choice on an ongoing basis.

13. Sponsor or subsidize children of employees to attend Christian camps.

14. Create support groups around specific topics such as parenting, saving money, or living missionally.

15. Initiate a morning huddle for prayer time and showcase a daily video for inspiration.

16. If your employees do not have family nearby, offer to cover the cost of babysitting services during a seminar, conference, or other development event that occurs outside regular working hours.

17. Sponsor and encourage employees and spouses to attend Family Life marriage seminars.

18. Give children's devotionals or Christian storybooks to employees for their children and grandchildren.

19. Lead a small group study or mentor individual employees on Christian values.

20. Organize company mission trips and assist employees in participating, shaping or even leading them.

21. Model application of Scripture in business. Look for teachable moments to use for illustrations.

22. Permit employees to do ministry on company time.

23. When giving out paychecks, write a personal note of appreciation or encouragement to each employee.

24. Sponsor employees to attend a Christian concert or seminar with a block of tickets.

25. Hold Conflict Resolution Training by Peacemakers as ways to invest in healthy culture, improve productivity levels, and also to infuse scriptural truths into a culture of peace.

26. Provide free pre-retirement counseling and planning seminars.

27. Make a list of names of family members of your employees with their ages, birthdays, anniversaries, or special interest, and send a scriptural note on special days. Encourage fellow employees to remember each other.

28. Chart direct report names and plot out a spiritual continuum. Commit to a strategy for determining where people are at and intentionally encouraging them towards next steps.

29. Maintain an emergency "deacon's fund," fueled by all employees and a small portion of net profits, to address occasional emergency needs of those in need/company stakeholders and rotate administration among teams of likeminded employees.

30. Actively encourage all team members to brainstorm and critique company activities and methods against stated biblical core principles.

31. Contract with local pastors or ministry leaders to do evangelism and discipleship equipping of staff.

32. Host topical lunch and learn gatherings on spiritual growth topics.

CLIENTS/CUSTOMERS/VENDOR MINISTRY

33. If hosting a weekly Bible study, invite clients to join in via video conference technology.

34. Host a Christ-centered movie event or provide theater tickets for vendor partners to see an upcoming show.

35. Have annual supplier and customer appreciation outings with a Kingdom message (e.g., testimonies, company purpose, gospel presentation, etc.).

36. Use special seasons (e.g., Christmas, Easter, Thanksgiving, New Year) to send cards or letters with tactful Gospel messages.

37. Host a supplier appreciation banquet to show them you value them as people.

38. Include tasteful evangelical tracts with invoices, payments, etc.

39. Have an annual supplier/customer open house to display and celebrate your company's Christian values and principles, share supportive stories from staff members, and recognize those who have exhibited what you promote.

40. Ask for prayer requests your company can pray about on their behalf.

41. Produce company-branded Gospels of John via Pocket Testament League for distribution to all guests.

MARKETING

42. Prepare a mission statement that identifies you as a Christian business with a ministry objective.

43. Design business cards and other collateral that clearly communicate your Christian values.

44. Share blogs and articles on LinkedIn with messages about incorporating ministry in business.

45. As a company, invite others to join in support of Christ-centered causes via social media.

46. Create and promote a video of your team on a ministry project to inspire others to join you.

47. Declare a uniquely Christian value to be expressed to customers and create a strategy around how sales, service, and production aim for and accomplish conveying that value to customers over the course of a year.

48. Utilize social media to reach new audiences with your message and mission.

49. Use Facebook or other tools to stream a sermon or motivational speech.

50. Tweet a daily Bible verse.

51. Develop an app to share business resources and biblical material.

52. Use your blog as a platform for truth sharing.

53. Start an e-newsletter with stories of changed lives in and through your organization.

54. Share video testimonies through a public YouTube channel.

55. Create your own social media challenge or contest to rally people around a specific Christian service initiative.

56. Create an opt-in daily text message distribution with an encouraging quote or Bible verse.

57. List your "credentials" as AfC (Ambassador for Christ) after your name on correspondence and business cards.

58. Sponsor a Christian radio program.

59. Provide business card sized coupons or discounts for employees to handout to bless others.

60. List Jesus Christ as owner of your business and you as steward on your letterhead.

61. Prepare several Christ-centered ways to answer the question, "What do you do for a living?"

WORK ENVIRONMENT

62. Play Christian music in your lobby, kitchen, or other common areas.

63. Institute a daily technology-free meditation and prayer time within the workday.

64. Place evangelistic self-service displays with literature (such as Gospels of John from The Pocket Testament League). Post follow-up options in lobbies, vending areas, and gathering spots.

65. Open and/or close company meetings with prayer and thanksgiving.

66. Have Christian magazines and a Bible in your waiting area.

67. Display Christian paintings, pictures, Scripture, etc.

68. Maintain a private counseling/devotional room with appropriate support materials.

69. Play a Christian station on your telephone system hold music.

70. Set up a prayer box for employees and patrons to submit requests.

71. Have a compassion resource or help-line directory in your office to guide those you come in contact with who may need directions in getting assistance.

72. Invite local pastors to come in or self-officiate periodic communion services before the start of a workday as an optional staff gathering.

73. Invite Christian motivational speakers to company meetings.

74. Setup ministry, mission, mercy, or compassion task forces or committees comprised of diverse employees to evaluate, select, and monitor ministry projects inside and outside the company.

75. Provide Christian worldview seminars open to the community.

76. Give away One-Year Bibles or other helpful study/application Bibles.

77. Use some of your firm's profits to support local ministries, especially those that help the poor.

78. When ordering food for company luncheons, consider ordering extra to be delivered to a local soup kitchen.

79. Provide company speakers/testimonials for local Kingdom and community events.

80. Hold community open houses to share with others what drives your business.

81. Hire disadvantaged people who have gone through a life-skills course and need employment.

82. Offer lodging and office space for visiting missionaries and traveling ministry workers.

83. Develop matching programs for staff who sponsor children or provide scholarships to good causes.

84. Actively solicit and refer prospective employees who resonate with your firm's distinctive passion and vision.

85. Provide discounted/free services to local pastors and other Christian leaders.

86. Lend your employees to a local ministry that needs administrative help.

87. Host a luncheon on Boss' Day or Administrative Professionals' Day in your marketplace and share your testimony.

88. Divide up annual charitable giving and allow employees to participate in the selection of where and how the money is distributed; then come together to celebrate/share stories from the giving project.

89. Conduct a drive for baby items for local pregnancy care centers. Throw a baby shower for one or more of the women committed to keeping her baby.

90. Assist struggling businesses in your vicinity as a mentor.

91. Collaborate with businesses in your area and host an appreciation banquet for the various compassion ministries in your community.

92. Donate computers or equipment to local after-school programs.

93. Pay your employees for time involved with a community outreach.

94. Host a lunch for local area pastors and church leadership.

95. Give away free stuff at events (bottled water, cold soda, gas) along with a care card that explains why you are doing it.

96. Enable local Kingdom ministries to use helpful company resources and infrastructure "at cost."

97. Provide practical internship and project opportunities for students, young pastors, and seminarians in need of experience and short-term income.

98. Sponsor a child overseas and ask your employees to serve as penpals, sending them letters on a monthly basis.

99. Sponsor a missionary, either domestically or overseas.

100. Give generously or tithe, based on company earnings, to worthy transformational projects in the community.

101. Sponsor missionary or service retreats for groups of employees who desire to minister as ambassadors for both Christ and your firm.

102. Sponsor youth athletic teams with uniforms and coaching that clearly promote Christian values. Host a season's end celebratory banquet.

Reprinted with permission from C12.

POLYDECK
CASE STUDY

The Polydeck Story: A Continuing Case Study in Workplace Caring

In 1993, following an advanced university education in Economics and a lifetime of mentoring from his Father, Peter Freissle joined the company founded by his father in South Africa in 1958. Political instability in South Africa actually resulted in Peter and his Dad being attacked and fired upon by armed gunmen on their way home. This prompted a decision in 1994 for Peter to move his family to Spartanburg, SC, where he became president of Polydeck Screen Corporation, a subsidiary founded by his Dad in 1978. Peter set out on what he thought was the America dream. His main goal, as for many company leaders, was to grow the business and make as much money as he could. He saw employees only as a means to help him make money. Employees would say they could hear Peter coming before he entered the room and would try to avoid any interaction with him if at all possible. An outside contracted employment agency actually stopped sending candidates to work at Polydeck due to complaints from applicants about the harsh and unpleasant work environment. This culture of fear was reflected in the 22% labor turnover rate. Little did Peter know that God knew exactly what was going on in his company and He had a plan for Peter. Although compartmentalized, Peter had a strong faith background but always drew a strong distinction between Faith and Work. This all changed in 2006 when Peter attended a silent retreat that would change his life forever.

At the Silent Spiritual retreat, God touched Peter's heart with intense love and mercy, and revealed a new paradigm to the Polydeck CEO. Prior to the retreat, Peter had been the center of his own focus, leaving only a tiny slice of his life for God. He knew if he truly wanted to put God in the center of his life, he would need to change and he would need to change how he ran his company. From that point forward, instead of seeing himself as the owner of the business, he realized that the business and the success he had achieved were gifts from God and that he was a steward of these gifts. He knew God would not ask "how much money did you make?" but He would ask "what Eternal value have you created with the talents and gifts I have given you?" This change in perspective helped Peter realize that God had given him this business to use as a platform for ministry and to spread God's message of Love with all those in his sphere of influence. He now understood that all of those in his sphere of influence were his neighbors and he needed to figure out how to love all of his neighbors like Jesus did.

Immediately following the retreat, Peter started by sharing his story with his Leadership Team. Over the next few months Peter, together with his executive team, crafted the new Vision for Polydeck which is to: Serve our customers and stakeholders with excellence and to achieve profitable growth which enables us to care for people in a way that honors God. He knew the ultimate Purpose of the company was "to create eternal value by striving to honor God in all we do." He then began sharing this new Vision and Purpose with all of the employees. He was on fire for the radical change God had burned in his heart and could not remain quiet on his new found Vision and Purpose. Of course, it was quite a shock for most of the team members at Polydeck and there were many skeptics waiting to see how this new initiative would play out.

Peter also worked with his Leadership Team to develop the mission statement (what did Polydeck do?) and the Core Values (how should Polydeck behave?). The Polydeck mission is to "Build upon our position as the leader in the screen media industry by partnering with our customers and using continuous improvement to provide optimal screening solutions, focusing on total Customer Satisfaction, Uncompromising Quality, Superior Service, Guaranteed Performance, Research and Development, and Unmatched Technical Support."

The Polydeck Core Values statement was formulated as "We are a company grounded on Christian values of humility, honesty, integrity, respect, kindness and a sense of social responsibility. We strive to create Eternal value in all that we do. These are reflected in how we conduct our business and how we care for our employees, who are our greatest asset."

Now it was time to develop the caring strategy for Polydeck. How was Polydeck going to live out the vision, purpose, mission and Core Values? Peter started by allocating 1% of company revenue for the caring budget and formed a Caring Team to decide how that money was to be used to enrich the lives and care for Polydeck employees and their families. As the company culture began to change with the introduction of caring programs that addressed physical needs, the Polydeck vision team introduced two company level caring initiatives vital for sustaining a caring company culture — a corporate chaplain and a place to pray. The corporate chaplain assures that each and every employee is ministered to on an individual basis. The chaplain makes rounds at the company weekly building caring relationships with employees while establishing trust. This trust allows the employees to confide in their chaplain during times of crisis and need. The chapel, affectionately known to Peter as 'his boss's office', provides a place to pray, a place for silence and meditation and a place for the chaplain to meet with employees and share resources as needed.

Polydeck created a Caring Team made up of employees representing different departments across the company, to help employees and their families see God's love through practical programs that help meet their physical, emotional/intellectual, and spiritual needs. The Caring Team becomes the eyes and ears of the company, helping to understand the needs and identifying Caring Activities to help meet the needs. The Caring Team started with a few relief funds. The first funds include a benevolent fund, a car repair fund, and a house repair fund and expanded activities over the next 8 years. In the physical needs category for employees, they offer a wellness program including an in house gym, medical screening, and sport teams. In the emotional/intellectual needs category, they offer financial budgeting, scholarships, addiction recovery, single parent support groups, training and education. In the spiritual needs category, they offer a resource library, weekly bible study with lunch, and prayer groups. In the family 'neighbor' category, they offer a family fun day at Carowinds, a family Christmas party and an Easter egg hunt for the employee's children on the company grounds. For the community 'neighbors', Polydeck encourages two hours of community service time from each employee. They also learn about, support and sponsor local non-profits voted on by the employees. As part of their international community caring strategy, Polydeck adopted a barrio in Nicaragua where employees can share their gifts and talents to help the barrio community become a self-sustaining community. The project is known as the Genesis project where Polydeck employees help the community build a local business, build a school, provide education on basic skills all while sharing the most important gift of love. Employees at Polydeck learned very quickly that they were not just there to serve but they were the one being served because of the love provided from each child and adult they worked with for the Genesis project.

In addition to planned Caring Activities, the real proof of a Caring Company Culture is when you begin to see employees caring for each other. Polydeck created a "Caught You Caring" program to allow fellow employees to recognize each other when they are caught living out their Core Values with each other. This program is shared in the monthly birthday and anniversary meeting held at Polydeck which includes an update on the company goals and results.

In 2014, Polydeck hired a Caring Company Culture Manager, Scott Gajewsky, former His Way at Work Executive Director, to ensure the proper resources were allocated to this important initiative. As the Caring Company Culture Manager, he was responsible for leading the Caring Team efforts, managing the company caring strategy budget and ensuring the Caring Activities are being implemented properly and successfully. This means active involvement with employees, their families and the community and a sense of understanding their needs. This role is also responsible for encouraging all leaders and supervisors to encourage their employees to be a part of the caring strategy AND to be the best caring leader they can be. Scott plays an integral role between the Leadership Team, the HR leader, the supervisors, the corporate chaplain, the employees, their families, and the community. Recently, the responsibility of Dream Manager was added to this role and Scott was certified as an official "Dream Manager" (inspired by Matthew Kelly's book The Dream Manager) and has started meeting with employees to help them formulate and reach their dreams.

At this point in the journey, it was important for Peter to answer the question: "are we living our purpose, mission and Core Values?" "Are we measuring what matters most?" The Leadership Team developed a "Balanced Scorecard" to help answer these questions. The scorecard was separated into two parts—Return on Investment (ROI) which is the typical way a company is measured, and Eternal Return on Investment (EternalROI™). EternalROI™ was a new concept for most people working for a traditional company. Examples of EternalROI™ metrics included Community service hours per employee, stewardship giving, core value index, employee satisfaction, employee turnover, % of employees that feel cared for during a time of personal crisis, number of employee involved in: cares sessions, hospital visits, marriage retreats, drug rehabilitation, mission trips, interest free loans, prayer group meetings and last but not least salvations.

As a result of implementing a Caring Strategy to support the purpose, mission and Core Values of Polydeck, Polydeck has been blessed with many successful results. Turnover went from 22% to 3% and revenue increased by 200%. As a result of employees feeling a connection and commitment to the culture of caring and the purpose of creating eternal value, they have engaged beyond merely receiving a paycheck and bring more enthusiasm and engagement to work each day, which has resulted in 10% increase in employee productivity. Even though this was not the ultimate reason for implementing a Caring Company Culture, all the company key metrics were moving in the right direction. The true and ultimate reason was to live out their Purpose to "serve their customers and stakeholders with excellence to achieve profitable growth which enables us to care for people in a way that honors God." Polydeck wanted to use their ROI to provide EternalROI™ for all their neighbors including their employees, their families and the community. The crowning result of all, because of the change God brought about in the company by encouraging Peter to come into true communion with Him, 80 people have accepted faith in Jesus Christ as their Lord and Savior! For this we give all glory and honor to God. Everyone recognizes the changes at Polydeck are a true work of God and not of man. Additionally, Peter knows other business leaders have similarly been touched by God to serve Him through the workplace and is encouraged to see more joining the ranks each and every day.

For more on the Polydeck story, download a copy of The Business Card book at *hwaw.com*.

BEST PRACTICES FROM THE JOURNEY OF FOUR CEOS

By Jeffrey Moore, Ph.D., Gustavo Cruz, MBA, and Armando Del Bosque, MBA.

Leaders in both private and public businesses are realizing that they can integrate their faith with their work and finding ways to do so. There actually is harmony between leading a business and serving God. His Way At Work (HWAW) has collaborated with Anderson University MBA program to research the common themes and relationships that four CEOs used in their EternalROI™ journey. Through a qualitative methodology Anderson University researchers interviewed the CEOs and their executives at four different companies in the Southeastern United States. The purpose of this study is to explore and understand the process of transforming a company from ROI centered to EternalROI™ oriented.

We bring four major findings that are: 1) CEO development in EternalROI™, 2) tools of culture change in EternalROI™ companies, 3) transformation phases of EternalROI™ companies, and 4) EternalROI™ company motto.

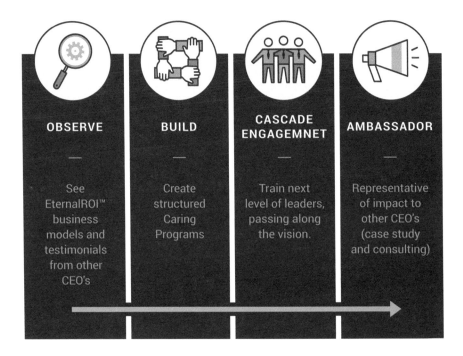

OBSERVE	BUILD	CASCADE ENGAGEMNET	AMBASSADOR
—	—	—	—
See EternalROI™ business models and testimonials from other CEO's	Create structured Caring Programs	Train next level of leaders, passing along the vision.	Representative of impact to other CEO's (case study and consulting)

CEOs start in a relatively (as they are usually already doing something) passive stage where they hear from other CEOs how business can have eternal significance. Each CEO discussed having a personal conviction and deep identity awakening to the importance of intentionally running the business according to God's principles. The active phase starts when the CEO takes the step (leap of Faith) and intentionally develops a carefully thought-out structure to support new or old caring programs that include a chaplain program, a caring committee and other caring activities.

In this stage the CEO is intentionally architecting the culture of the organization to embrace this change. The third stage is having the next level of leadership starts becoming the champions of the culture change. Finally the ambassador stage is when the CEO goes and speaks to outside stakeholders sharing his testimony about the EternalROI™ culture transformation and positive impact in transforming lives.

TOOLS OF CULTURE CHANGE IN ETERNALROI™ COMPANIES

Tool 4:
RAISING NEXT LEVEL OF LEADERS

Employees demonstrate
ownership in organization.

Focus on leadership
cascade engagement, serving
others and operational excellence

Tool 3:
FOCUSING ON SIGNIFICANCE AND LIVING CORE VALUES

Active engagement by employees.
We care about each other.

Freedom to make decisions
in caring committee.
Internalizing and "being" the values.
Leveraging business stressors.

Tool 2:
DEVELOPING EMPLOYEES

Low active engagement
by employees.

Focus on technical and
soft skill development.

Tool 1:
CREATING CARING PROGRAMS

Passive engagement by employees.
CEO caring about employee.

Focus on introducing
new programs.

CEOs use four common tools to influence culture change in their companies. The first tool is the **creating caring programs** starting with the chaplain program and caring committee. Here the CEO is showing his/her care for his/her employees. The second tool is **developing employees:** the professional development of the employee to address lower motivational needs of the employee such as physical, safety and technical skill improvement which leads to promotion and higher pay. Without addressing these lower order needs, employees are not able to progress to engagement, feeling part of team, even reaching to mutual actualization. The third tool is **focusing on significance** and making a difference in the life of others and each other. At this time the caring committee is being completely governed by the employees. The final tool is **raising the next level of leadership** to live out servant leadership while driving operational excellence.

BECOMING AN ETERNALROI™ COMPANY:
FOCUS STAGES OF ORGANIZATIONAL CHANGE.

METRICS STAGE *Profit Focus*	TRANSITION STAGE *Learning Focus*	ETERNALROI™ STAGE *Eternal Investment Focus*
FOCUS		
Reacting to **business pressures**	Developing **Caring Programs** (activities)	Honoring God by living the Core Values and Purpose
CORE VALUES		
Maximize **profitability**	**Struggle** to balance business pressures with developing people	**Develop employees** while increasing operational excellence. Employee owned caring activities (physical, emotional and spiritual)
LEADERSHIP STYLE		
Top down leadership	Learning to lead (executive team) by **example** and with **humility**. Balance care for employee with professional standard of excellence	**Servant leadership:** How can I serve you to make you successful in achieving your job goals?
CHALLENGE		
High employee turnover, untapped opportunities (cost, waste, productivity, creativity...), **no employee engagement**	Establish a clear and thorough culture change process with communication strategy "2 years intead of 7" **Danger of ineffective culture change**	**Maintain and sustain culture.** Drive culture down to all levels

The first stage of the company is an ROI focus where metrics based on profit are the central focus and it is constantly reacting to business pressures. Leadership tends to be top down where a leader leads out of ego or fear. Executives we interviewed talked about high employee turnover and untapped opportunities because employees were not engaged. The second stage is a transitional phase where the CEO and his/her team struggle with balancing business pressures and the caring programs. What is the line between caring and expecting excellence in quality and production/service? During this time the organization is learning by trial and error unless it is engaged into a structured change management process like His Way At Work, learning to apply its new values. The third stage is an EternalROI™ stage where the business is driven by the desire to honor God and live out their Core Values. The leadership style turns to employee focused management (Moore, Hanson, Maxey & Kraemer, 2015). The challenge is to maintain the culture, driving it down to all levels of the organization. To that end, a robust change management program should be in place, including a comprehensive communication strategy.

In summary we understand the EternalROI™ company motto to be: "Committed to loving employees and operational excellence!" CEOs and their teams report that balancing caring for employees with expecting performance excellence. In all these cases the culture was transformed by the passion of the CEO to love God and love others, starting with the closest neighbor—employees. The CEO and team, balance caring and developing employees who go beyond compliance, focused on improving quality, being innovative, exceeding production standards and exceeding customer expectations.

Reprinted with permission from Jeff Moore.

References:
Moore, J., Hanson, W., Maxey E., Kraemer, L. (2015). Fully Integrated Inclusive Organization: Beyond Accommodations. Paper presented at Academy of Management conference in Vancouver, BC.

BIBLIOGRAPHY

Jacobs, Buck. *A Light Shines In Babylon.* 4th ed., The C12 Group, LLC.

O'Steff, Steve. *The Business Card Book.* Lanphier Press, 2015.

Lencioni, Patrick. *The Five Dysfunctions of a Team: Team Assessment.* San Francisco, Pfeiffer, 2007.

Lencioni, Patrick. *The Advantage: Why Organizational Health Trumps Everything Else in Business.* San Francisco, Jossey-Bass, 2012.

Qualfon. *Answering the Call.* 1st ed., Qualfon, 2015.

Blanchard, Kenneth H., Phil Hodges, and Phyllis Hendry. *Lead like Jesus Revisited: Lessons from the Greatest Leadership Role Model of All Time.* Nashville, TN: W Group, an Imprint of Thomas Nelson, 2016.